Get a Better Job!

Ed Rushlow

Peterson's Guides

Princeton, New Jersey

Material from *Psycho-cybernetics* by Maxwell Maltz, M.D., F.I.C.S., copyright © 1960, is used by permission of the publisher, Prentice-Hall, Inc., Englewood Cliffs, New Jersey.

Excerpts from "You Can't Roller Skate in a Buffalo Herd" by Roger Miller, copyright © 1964, Tree Publishing Co., Inc., are used by permission of the publisher. All rights reserved. International copyright secured.

Excerpts from "Ac-cent-tchu-ate The Positive," lyric by Johnny Mercer, music by Harold Arlen, copyright © 1944 Harwin Music Co., © renewed 1972 Harwin Music Co., are used by permission of the publisher. All rights reserved. International copyright secured.

Library of Congress Cataloging-in-Publication Data

Rushlow, Ed, 1924–
    Get a better job! / Ed Rushlow.
        p.   cm.
    ISBN 0-87866-955-8
    1. Job hunting. I. Title.
HF5382.7.R87   1990
650.14—dc20
                                                    90-31382
                                                    CIP

Composition and design by Peterson's Guides

Printed in the United States of America

10 9 8 7 6 5 4 3 2 1

This book is dedicated to you.

ABOUT THE AUTHOR

Ed Rushlow has managed his own executive recruiting and consulting firm, serving Fortune 500 companies. He was a combat pilot during World War II and has been Sales Manager for the General Electric Missile and Space Vehicle Department, Vice President of Marketing for the CONRAC Corporation, Division General Manager of the NARMCO Materials Division of the Whittaker Corporation, Vice President of Marketing and International Operations for Baker Oil Tools, and President of SCI International.

He graduated cum laude with a B.S. in Chemical Engineering from the University of New Hampshire and has an M.S. in Nuclear Chemistry and Physics from Ohio State. He now consults for Rushlow & Company, the recruiting firm managed by his wife, Peggy. He and Peggy reside in Inverness, Florida.

Contents

(continued)

Preface

My avocation is hang gliding. I learned the sport when it was in its infancy. We were all beginners, and there were no instructors. Learning was by trial and error: you hooked up to the kite and ran down a slope in hopes of becoming airborne. If you did not succeed, you crashed on knees and elbows. If you did, you crashed on landing, but at least you had the satisfaction of having flown.

Though there were no instructors, we never lacked coaches. The bystanders provided a steady flow of advice based on the expertise they gained by watching. Most of us persisted and did learn. On my twenty-fifth run with the kite, I "joined the big guys" and launched myself from the 500-foot hill.

In the early days of the sport, we recorded flights of a few minutes. Since then, I've flown over 4 hours, reached 9,000 feet, and covered 30 miles cross-country (not big numbers compared to those achieved by today's experts). Today, beginners hook up and take off from 5,000-foot mountains after their first few tries and are soon "skying out" on thermals, gaining thousands of feet of altitude. The difference? They are taught by someone who has been there.

When I first entered the job market some forty years ago, I suffered the equivalent of hang-gliding bruises, not to my knees or elbows but to my ego. I was no different from anyone else. None of us had been taught anything about the art of finding a job. As in hang gliding, I barged ahead using trial and error.

I waded through the rejections, embarrassments, uncertainties, and mysteries of job search. Books offered advice, but none of the authors had spent significant time in the job-search trenches. They were bystanders: personnel directors, employment agents, psychiatrists, psychologists, recruiters, placement directors, etc. Their theories did not match my experiences.

Later, when I became a recruiter, I met hundreds of candidates. Since they, too, had no teachers who had been where they were going, their approaches to a new career were by trial and error also. That was when I decided to write this book, for I knew that I could speed you on to the better job of your choice.

All that is needed is here, it's all based on experience in the trenches, and it's all for you. Hook up and soar the thermals to your better job.

Ed Rushlow
March 1990

Your Comments Will Be Appreciated

Please join me in improving the fortunes of those entering the trenches of job search by contributing to subsequent editions of *Get a Better Job!* Send your comments, suggestions, criticisms, and corrections to:

F. E. Rushlow
P.O. Box 644
Inverness, FL 32651-0644

Chapter 1

Help Yourself to a Better Job

"You have more capability to bring to the job market than you may realize or be willing to admit."

This book is going to help you get a better job. It is written for people who are actively seeking new jobs or new careers, for those who are just beginning to think seriously about the possibility of making a change, and for those who aren't yet thinking about changing but are still dissatisfied with their present jobs. Recent graduates will also find the book very helpful in landing a better *first* job. Those of you whose only need is to create the impression of looking for a job can leave it lying around as a prop so others will think you're hard at work.

The advice I have to offer applies to managers, to supervisors, and to the individual contributors who do their jobs with no interest in supervising others—in other words, to *all* of you. No matter who you are, you have unique talents to contribute. The techniques you are going to learn work because they come from actual experience in the job market: mine. Forget about theory and forget about magic and luck. You won't need them.

You're already familiar with some of the **tools** you'll need to get a better job: a telephone, a typewriter or word processor, and a resume. You will learn to use a network of helpers. The **pathways** you will take to a better job involve the contributions of friends and associates, as well as the use of letters, job advertisements, recruiters, and employment applications. You'll learn all about these tools and pathways in the following chapters. It will not be the sort of theoretical training that comes from someone who has never practiced what he preaches, nor will it be based on the observations of someone sitting on the sidelines. I have tested all these techniques

1

in my thirty-plus years in the job trenches. They have worked for me, and I know how to get them to work for you.

It's Do-It-Yourself Time

If your plumbing needs repairing, you have a choice. You can hire a plumber or you can do it yourself. Not true when it comes to a job search. You can't hand this responsibility off. The only practical approach is to run with it yourself. You'll be supported by the techniques you learn here.

Beware! There are firms that will tell you they can do the work for you. They will promise to speed you to your new career by writing your resume, "shrinking your head," putting you through charm school, bringing out your fine points, grooming you for interviews, arranging meetings, etc. Paying them to do this is like hiring someone to go on a diet for you. You don't need these services. After reading Chapter 6, where you get the lowdown on these outfits, you'll want to avoid them altogether.

Some people would have you believe that you can run a confidential job search through a friend or even through a hired hand. They suggest an approach something like this:

> "I know a very well qualified person who would like to make a career change. She is experienced in thus and so and has accomplished this and that. Would you like to hire her?"

This doesn't work. In the first place, there is no such thing as a confidential job search (more on that later). And what friend has the time to conduct an effective campaign on your behalf? You will most likely end up with no new job, having overworked the friendship or bought your hired hand a new Mercedes in the process.

The only way to go is on your own. This is not a blanket endorsement of doing it yourself. If you have never plastered a ceiling, don't—at least not in your own home. This is, however, a blanket put-down of go-betweens. Just remember what happened in pilgrim times when John Alden asked Priscilla for her hand, not for himself but for Miles Standish. Priscilla's reply was one of history's best one-liners: "Speak for yourself, John" (with credits to Henry Wadsworth Longfellow, of course). I don't believe any intermediary can be effective on your behalf. But he or she could win the job you're after.

It Takes Some Effort

The effort you put into your job search will depend on your "urgency factor," as illustrated here, and on the level of the career target you're aiming for. If you are secure in your present position or have private means and don't need a job urgently, you can spend fewer hours a week looking for a job than if you are out of work and savings with a family to support. In the latter case, job search becomes a 60-hour-a-week job. Your own urgency factor probably falls somewhere in between these extremes. But remember this: the effort you invest in doing a job search in the right way will pay dividends for life.

Urgency Factor

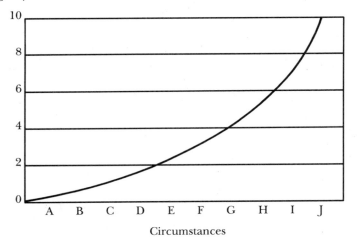

Circumstances

    A. Private means of support
    B. Willing to move for a 50 percent increase in salary
    C. Would move for "just the right job"
    D. Would like to live somewhere else
    E. Passed over for promotion
    F. Domineering and disruptive boss
    G. Company acquired and future in doubt
    H. Company involved in unethical business practices
    I. Company in bankruptcy
    J. Out of a job and out of savings, with a family to support

The level of your job target will also influence the amount of work you need to put into landing a new job. It will take fewer hours to capture a position as a supervisor than one as a manager simply because there are fewer managerial jobs, and they are more difficult to find. The higher you are on the career ladder, the more effort you'll have to put into your job search.

The more you work at it, the sooner you'll have a choice of jobs you really like. However, I have found that many who want and/or need a new position just putter around until any old job comes along. They follow a path of little resistance. A good example is the job hunter who depends entirely on mailing out resumes. This approach reminds me of the carpenter who lost his hammer outside but looked for it in the house because it was warmer there.

My company does executive search under contract for client companies, recruiting candidates to fill assigned positions. As a "public service," I also help local unemployed people who do not fit existing searches, giving them tips on how to get a successful job search under way. Only one in four of the people I counsel is willing to make the effort needed to find the right job. The rest seem content to take whatever comes their way, even when this sometimes means not finding a job at all.

In fairness to most of those whose job search is only halfhearted, I believe their lack of effort stems from a state of depression. A person out of work feels serious rejection; depression sets in and inaction results. Some sink so low they consider themselves unemployable and give up. The symptoms are usually a brave front and minimal effort: mailing out a few copies of a poorly written resume, making futile trips to the mailbox, and sitting back to wait for the ideal offer.

The antidote to this depressed, nonproductive condition is to apply *energy*, to put the steps in this book into action. The more effort you put into it, the sooner you'll find yourself with the enviable task of choosing among several attractive opportunities. Believe me, the tools and pathways work. Reading this book works. But someone must turn the crank, and that someone is you. As you read this book you'll find yourself getting into it, and your job search will become something you want to spend time on, a real confidence builder.

Learn from the examples of two job hunters who made the effort and came out on top—and two who waited for that better job that never came.

The Financial Manager Who Wouldn't Work

Consider the case of Thomas Felder, a financial manager who came to my office under the "public service" program. He had been referred by an acquaintance. He was 42 years old, had a wife and child, and owned his own home. He had received an M.B.A. from Notre Dame in 1968. Tom had been in his last position for six years and was earning over $57,000 a year when he left. It was his third job since getting his M.B.A. This was the profile of an excellent candidate.

In spite of this, Tom had been out of a job for ten months. It was not clear why he had left his old company, but it was clear why he had not connected since. He was not working the problem. He came to me hoping I had a position waiting just for him, even though it had been clear up front that this was not the case. Once he had established that I really had no job for him, he stopped paying attention. His attitude seemed to be, "If you don't have a job for me, please don't bother me with details." The one version of his resume he was using was off the mark, yet he would not accept suggestions. He claimed to have taken all the steps I described to him, but it was apparent that, at best, his had been the token effort of sending out a few of these inadequate resumes. Tom took no notes during our session and seemed to slough off advice. It was apparent that he had no interest in putting some effort into looking for a better job, and, as far as I know, he is still out of work.

The Recovering Alcoholic Who Did Work

Joseph Knoll was sent to me by a mutual friend. He was 30 and was married with three children. A high school graduate, Joe had earned $6.25 per hour at his last job. He had just been through a twenty-eight-day alcohol recovery program and was now a member of Alcoholics Anonymous. Although he was very intelligent and alert, he was suffering from very low self-esteem and the fear that he was unemployable. He listened closely as I gave him a quick rundown on how to find a job, and he gained confidence as we talked. We were able to set job targets that fit his background, experience, and desires.

Joe had waited on tables, worked in a car wash, parked cars, and delivered early morning papers. These can all be tough and thankless jobs, and that Joe stuck with them showed me he was not afraid of hard work. He had also sold consumer goods at the retail level and took pride in his successes as a salesman.

We structured two resumes that capitalized on his assets: his willingness to work and his ability to sell. One aimed at inside sales and the other at marketing products and services to businesses. An inside sales position involving the servicing of orders and the handling of customer complaints would pay near entry level but would get him in on the ground floor of a company where he could move up. Marketing products and services such as telephone systems, janitorial services, copying equipment, or computer time would give him an opportunity to earn more through commissions.

Joe applied himself diligently. He reported back on his activities and his progress, describing the number of calls made, resumes sent, letters written, etc. He checked in before each interview for last-minute advice. Within two weeks, Joe had three solid offers. He accepted one in business marketing. His approach had so impressed the company that he was offered both salary and commission in a position that usually paid commission only.

Joe worked. What I taught him worked.

The College Graduate Who Waited for a Job to Find Him

Dennis Price was 30 years old and worked as a clerk in the electronics department of a retail store, earning just above the minimum wage. He was married, had two children, and owned his own home. He had a bachelor's degree from the University of Maine. He was well groomed and articulate, and he seemed to have a style that worked with customers. One day when my wife bought a calculator in his department and paid with a company check, Dennis noticed the company name and asked the nature of the business. The conversation ended with Dennis accepting an offer of job counseling.

He had been in his present job about a year. Prior to that he had worked as a contract administrator for a large electronics firm for five years, earning an annual salary of $28,000. After we talked awhile, I concluded that Dennis probably had lost that job due to a disagreement with his management. I could not decide if it was laziness or loss of confidence that kept Dennis in the electronics department.

Dennis was another one of those who hoped that I would have a challenging position just waiting for him. As the realization sunk in that I didn't, he slouched in his chair and listened with marginal politeness. He left armed with a new resume and the very strong advice that with proper effort he would soon be on a more promising career path.

Three months later I met Dennis at his same old job. He acknowledged that he had done nothing toward improving his career. I concluded that Dennis subconsciously felt defeated by whatever had happened at the contract administration job and, rather than risk more of the same, had decided to remain moored in a safe harbor. I would have liked to help, but neither I nor anyone else could do the work for him.

The Friend Who Made a Successful Career Change

Susan Barrett, a friend from church, was 34, single, and had an executive job with the county that paid $55,000 a year and included among its perks a car, an expense account, worldwide travel, and a bonus. She had a B.S. in marketing from California State University, Northridge, and an M.B.A. from UCLA. She owned an attractive condo. Everything seemed to be going her way when the administration changed, and she ended up unemployed without severance pay. We spent several sessions together.

Sue's specialty was marketing the tourist facilities of our area. It was obvious that, if she was to continue in this field, a move would be necessary. She decided instead to make a career change. Having enjoyed a $55,000 salary, she had the overhead to match it and could not afford to be out of work for long. Job search became her new, 50-hour-a-week task, and she implemented all the techniques I taught her. It was not easy for Sue, and at one point she had to arrange with her bank for a moratorium on her mortgage payments. She was tempted on two occasions to take that "next job that comes along" but persisted. In the end, she had the choice of two positions that would capitalize on her marketing skills. She gave some on compensation but gained in not having to relocate and no longer working in an environment subject to political changes.

For every story of work and success like Sue's there are at least three of job hunters who just stumbled along, taking whatever job happened to be offered or remaining unemployed for months.

Words of Wisdom

The Great Guru on Career Mountain says, "Ad-lib a job search and you'll end up with whatever comes down the pike. Discipline yourself to skillfully apply the techniques in this book and you'll win the job of your choice." Following are four golden rules that will help you get a better job with the minimum necessary expenditure of time and energy.

Stay on the Payroll

Often, people will stomp off the job in a huff only to find themselves eating into their savings while scrambling for the next paycheck. When you are not working, you lose much of your leverage in negotiating compensation. Quitting ends up being a very expensive ego trip. Write it in your hat so you won't forget:

NEVER, NEVER, NEVER QUIT YOUR PRESENT JOB
UNTIL YOU HAVE THE NEXT ONE.

Fight Procrastination

Procrastination will undermine your efforts. Commit yourself to a plan and a schedule; then stick to them. On-again, off-again attempts to get a better job will result in a weak campaign. Besides, the longer you are at a job search the greater the chance your resume will end up on your boss's desk, and that could present a problem. So remember:

BEAT PROCRASTINATION WITH A PLAN AND A SCHEDULE.

Set Reasonable Targets

Don't undershoot or overshoot—go for your level of competence.

You have more capability to bring to the job market than you may realize or be willing to admit. One of my goals is to show you how easy it is to identify and win job opportunities, provided you save your humility for another time.

By all means aim high, but fight the tendency to aim too high. Job hunters often hope for a grand promotion. This might happen if you're in the happy position of having a company come after you, but when you're out in the job market on your own, be realistic. Don't aim beyond the capability you have demonstrated in the past.

For example, general management seems to be a popular target for those who have never done it. Face it, companies get general managers from the stock they have been grooming from within or pick someone from outside who has a documented track record in general management. Before targeting this or any other new career, make sure you are qualified. A trusted friend who knows your work can help by offering an informed opinion as to whether your targets are realistic. Don't forget:

SHOOT FOR A REALISTIC CAREER LEVEL.

Don't Run a Cut-Rate Campaign

The most cost-effective job campaign involves jumping in and getting it done. This may not be a critical consideration if you are under no pressure. It becomes so when you are unemployed, "on the beach." Then you have to get a job regardless of the cost. You will recover the money you spend on your job campaign many times over simply by getting a paycheck sooner.

I've counseled many unemployed people who, out of concern for their dwindling resources, skimp on the cost of their job search. Denying yourself the use of secretarial help, printing, word processing, mail services, Federal Express, fax and telephone facilities, and travel is a foolish economy anytime you're looking for a job. But when you're eating up savings it becomes absurd. You've got to spend money to make money. Besides, you are after an important prize. So, whatever you do:

DON'T RUN A SKIMPY CAMPAIGN.

The First Step

The most difficult part of the process is getting started. You've already done that by reading this far. Now you're ready to move on to the next chapter and the first step in your campaign. By now I'm sure you've guessed that it's going to be the preparation of 100 copies of your new resume. Right? WRONG!

Chapter 2

Your Objective

"Sound, logical career goals are there waiting for you."

You are after the new job of your choice. You don't want to end up like many others, simply taking a job because it's available. A practical goal for you is to be able to select from among three positions that fit your objectives. You will reach this goal through interviews with the only ones who can say, "Hire this person," and make it stick—the Decision Makers (DMs). And you will gain access to DMs by using the tools and following the pathways mentioned in Chapter 1 and discussed in detail in later chapters.

I'm going to teach you proven techniques for winning job offers and give you pointers that will set you apart from the rest of the crowd in the job market. The reason that sending out 100 copies of your resume is not the first step will become obvious as we proceed. For now, suffice it to say that you will be supporting your campaign with various versions of your resume, not just one. The first step in the job search is the most important.

THE FIRST STEP IS TO SET YOUR CAREER GOALS.

Have you ever found yourself at the supermarket, wondering what you came for? You can call home, trying to disguise your forgetfulness, or go back outside and start again. It's annoying, but no harm is done. However, to end up in the job market without knowing why you're there is just plain foolish. You must set your objectives and keep them clearly before you.

If a mental barrier just tried to come down, control it. We all know that setting aside routines, distractions, and leisure activities in favor of planning seems to go against human nature. In fact, human nature would probably rather wing it. Do yourself a favor

10

and save "winging it" for your next vacation or trip to the racetrack. Admittedly, setting career goals is not the most exciting activity. It may appear to be difficult, particularly if you have been in the career melee for some time. The straight truth is that if you spend a few hours thinking about where you want to go with your career—sacrificing an evening of TV or a night out—your odds of getting there will improve tremendously. Planning your career is really not that difficult. You will find the simple steps that follow both enlightening and enjoyable.

Criteria for Goal Setting

The criteria are simple. Your goals must:

- Match the employment market.
- Be supported by your background and experience.

It would be unrealistic to strive for a job as corporate poet, since there are few openings. It would be impractical to pursue a job as an airline pilot when you've never flown a plane.

To match your goals to the market, it is important to realize that the emphasis today is on specialization. If they can, companies always fill an open position with someone who is experienced in their products or services. This truth is borne out in my executive search business. When client companies come to me seeking candidates to fill key openings, the first question I ask is, "Who are your competitors?" The answer reveals where the successful candidate can be found. Clients want someone who will be working up to speed from the first day. To find this person, the recruiter strives to fill a specification that includes the function to be performed *and* the products or services involved. Here are some examples of functions matched to their products and services:

Function	Products/Services
Salesman	Broad goods
Design engineer	Automotive suspension
Machinist	Space shuttle components
Nurse	Intensive care
Manufacturing manager	Plastic pipe
Pilot	767s
Architect	Hospitals
Finance manager	Property development
Chief executive	Mainframe computers

No effort will be made to present candidates from other backgrounds until the recruiter has exhausted all those from sources with matching products or services. This demonstrates emphatically that the most effective approach to the job market is to display your talents in terms not only of functions served but also of appropriate product and service experience. The closer your campaign matches market needs, the sooner you will be launched in your new job.

Specialization

Twenty-five years ago, specialization was not as important as it is today. One could enter the job market as a generalist, presenting functional experience alone with little reference to products or services. An employer would decide on the basis of the candidate's general background whether he or she was likely to be of use to the company.

One of the most successful career counselors at that time was Carl R. Boll. As employment adviser to the Harvard Business School Alumni Association and as author of *Executive Jobs Unlimited,* he helped thousands of job seekers. The Boll approach involved composing a resume and letter based on functional specialties, such as marketing, finance, engineering, sales, public relations, manufacturing, and so on, that would apply to a wide range of companies. He recommended that 100 mailings be made each week in a shotgun-style approach. Boll reported a success rate of from 4 to 6 percent; that is, 4 to 6 interviews resulted from every 100 letters.

This so-called "broadcast letter" campaign does not work today. I know, for I have sent out hundreds of letters in the best Boll tradition without getting one meaningful interview. A standard letter and resume cannot zero in on specialized targets. Happily, we have a tool in today's word processor that allows us to put away the shotgun and use a rifle, easily matching both function and product specialties to particular job targets.

My stress on specialization does not mean that it is impossible to switch products or services. Under special circumstances, people are hired who still have something to learn about the job. Before he did so, Peter Ueberroth had never managed an Olympics or been commissioner of baseball. My friend Susan decided that staying in our community was more important to her than relocating in another town to pursue her specialty of marketing local tourist attractions. She opted to change her product line, becoming sales manager for a cellular phone company. It took longer to connect, and she accepted a lower compensation level, but she understood that these were the prices she must pay for her decision.

However, the quickest way to a new job is to highlight your specific background and experience as they match your target company's product line. When it comes to filling key positions, the employer's first choice is people who are experienced in the specialties involved in those positions. Except when hiring at entry level or when growing from within, companies usually shy away from on-the-job training.

Avoiding Pitfalls

Setting career goals can become a full-time career in itself. If setting goals paid a decent wage, you wouldn't need to worry. However, in the real world, overplanning merely extends your period of underemployment or unemployment. There are many theoretical treatments of the subject of setting career goals; in fact, one of the most popular books on job search spends so much time on goal setting that it never does get to the work of job finding. There are as many pitfalls to be avoided as there are theories. Let's look at some of them in detail.

The Search for Perfection

Wemble Smiff worked in my division. He was a perfectionist and was never able to bring any project to what he thought was a satisfactory conclusion. He was always on the verge of completing something and conscientiously called at all hours of the day and night to report on his progress. He was a manager's nightmare, but when I heard that corporate staff was looking for a planner, I gave Smiff a glowing recommendation and he got the job. Through sheer management skill, I killed three birds with one stone. Smiff's move improved the quality of both corporate staff and my division, while it furthered company performance. Wemble kept corporate staff planning and planning and planning to such a high standard that it had little time to harass the operating divisions, which then had the time to get the job done.

Perfectionism can be just as counterproductive in a job search as in the workplace. Avoid trying to define the absolutely perfect job or job campaign. You don't need a vernier when you're measuring yards, and your job yardstick should not be so finely calibrated that you rule out many good possibilities. Perfection, as we all know, is impossible to find.

Excessive Detail

Looking for a job that meets very precise specifications is similar in effect to a craving for perfection: you may find yourself out of time with an impractical target. Consider my friend who decided to buy a car. After long and meticulous consideration, he defined his goal as follows:

> A Volkswagen
> A Scirocco
> Gray
> Yellow stripe
> Five-speed
> Moonroof
> Lambskin seat covers
> Mermaid hood ornament
> No cigarette lighter
> AM/FM radio with cassette and CD players

Six months after setting these goals, he reported from Frankfurt on the great beer, Wiener schnitzel, and schnapps and said he had a hot lead on the exact car in Munich. You can make the same mistake in a job search, setting a target so specific that it will be extremely difficult if not impossible to reach.

The Couch, the Computer, and the Questionnaire

Chapter 6 looks in detail at the work of career counselors and the psychologists they employ. Here I just want to say that, unless you are trying to discover your general aptitudes, you won't need any psychological services when setting your job goals.

These days, the old psychological tests are turning up on computer software, but don't be fooled into thinking they have more credibility because of that. The questions are the same, but you use a keyboard rather than a pencil, and the evaluator has an automatic system for tallying your score.

Excellent computer-based programs do exist to help explore aptitudes that are not obvious or are yet to be defined. These are useful for students deciding on a career path and for those forced into a radical career change. The system in Florida is called Choices, is sponsored by the Department of Education, and is available to anyone willing to take the time to use it. If you are unsure whether to sail your USS *Career* north, south, east, or west, these computer programs are great for identifying broad career areas that fit your basic configuration. Go for it. Otherwise, you've got everything you need to launch your search without such aids.

Then there are the multiple-choice questionnaires that promise to help you analyze your character and chart your course. Numerical scores are related to aptitudes, talents, tendencies, etc. Following is an example from a popular questionnaire measuring life expectancy:

	A	**B**	**C**
Do you fasten your seat belt?	Always	Sometimes	Never
What is your cholesterol count?	150	200	250
Do you use alcohol?	Never	Moderately	Heavily
Are you overweight?	No	10 pounds	20 pounds

Answers in column A get 5 points, those in B get 3, and those in C get 1. You add up all the points, and the total is supposed to be how long you are going to live. I'm going to reach age 99 if I start living up to all the column A answers I gave.

Unveiling Your Goals

Sound, logical career goals are there waiting for you. Now's the time to learn how to unveil them. It's a simple process in which you can do most of the thinking while commuting, jogging, relaxing in the bath, etc. All you have to do is bring to light the data you already have. You will end up with several targets, and you will choose from these as you match your efforts to particular opportunities at hand. Your objectives will be based on four lists that summarize your background and experience in different ways:

- **Employment.** This is a record of all your significant employment. No need to remember such particulars as how long a job lasted, what it paid, the boss's name, or even the company's name. The purpose here is to jog your memory for what is to come.
- **Functions.** This is a list of all the roles you have played in the positions mentioned on your employment record. It serves as an inventory of your functional credentials.
- **Products and Services.** On this list, you record all the products and services that are within your work experience. Spend plenty of time compiling a comprehensive rundown that will make the widest sweep possible.
- **Accomplishments.** This is your brag sheet. In it you describe your most significant achievements.

Let the Results Simmer

Having completed your first round of list making, you can put the exercises aside and let your conscious and subconscious mind review the past for valuable data you may have overlooked. Then go back to your lists and add the important input you have received while counting sheep, daydreaming, people watching, weight lifting, etc. It is not an exercise you can do "by the numbers." Relax and let it happen. You will be rewarded for going the extra mile, because adding to your product and service repertoire and amplifying your list of accomplishments will expand the horizons of your job opportunities.

Jennifer Sets Her Goals

Jennifer Rhodes is 28 years old and lives in Los Angeles, where she owns a condo. She is not married, and is not contemplating it in the near future. She holds a B.A. from the University of Vermont, where she majored in business administration and minored in health care. She is pursuing her M.B.A. at night at Southern Cal. Jennifer has been with Madison's Department Store for four years and now earns $32,000 a year as a senior buyer in jewelry. Prior to that she spent three years in retail sales at Bronk's. Her first job out of college was with a local orthodontist.

Jennifer does well as a buyer, having had three very successful lines last year. She feels her career advancement is blocked by her boss, who has been with the store for ten years and will probably be in the same job for another ten. He and Jennifer have worked well together, but she has already learned most of what she can from him. Through one of the salespeople who call on her, Jennifer has become familiar with the life-style, level of compensation, and career paths available in field sales. She decides to explore the possibilities.

Jennifer's first three goal-setting lists look like this:

Employment
High school
Restaurant
Dental office
Department stores

Functions
Tutor
Hostess
Dental assistant
Retail salesperson
Retail sales supervisor, directing the activities of other salespeople and performing such management functions as

employee motivation, performance appraisal, inventory control, loss prevention, and so on
Buyer

Products and Services
Tutored juniors and seniors in math and algebra
Served as hostess for a gourmet restaurant specializing in traditional New England fare (part-time in high school and college)
Assisted an orthodontist
Sold cosmetics and jewelry
Sold and supervised the selling of watches and jewelry

When it came to listing her accomplishments, I gave Jennifer these instructions:

> Your aim is to establish *special* job goals. You do this by mulling over your career data to select the accomplishments in which you take the most pride. This is essential to a rifle-shot offensive, for identifying these achievements gives you two important inputs: it tells you *what you like to do* and *what you do best*. These two are impeccable criteria for the selection of a new job. Spend some time at this task. For each position held, briefly describe the accomplishments that gave you the most satisfaction. They may be things no one else knows about. It makes no difference. The important consideration is your pride in having done them. Record also the things that gave you the greatest feeling of self-esteem. Jot down your thoughts, and lay your work aside for later revision and re-revision. Let your conscious and subconscious mind sift the data until you can be proud of the list itself.

This resulted in her fourth and final goal-setting list:

Accomplishments
Helped nine out of ten students tutored improve their math grades
Cordially greeted restaurant patrons under all circumstances and developed an extensive clientele who made reservations only through me
Efficiently assisted the dentist, but otherwise accomplished nothing

Recorded the highest sales volume per hour of floor time in the cosmetic department by developing repeat business from satisfied customers

Became the youngest sales supervisor in the country for the Elson line of fine cosmetics

Was recruited from Bronk's by Madison's Department Store on the basis of my reputation for achievement

As a buyer, was able to increase volume and profit by picking lines with broad customer appeal and respectable margins

Jennifer's instructions for the final goal-setting step were as follows:

> When you have inventoried your accomplishments thoughtfully, the next task is to choose the ones that stand out and are of the most significance to your new-job campaign. The functions that correspond to your chosen accomplishments can now be combined with *any* of your product or service specialties to form specific career goals.

Jennifer had performed the functions of tutor/instructor, hostess, dental assistant, salesperson, supervisor, and buyer. She had product and service experience in mathematics, restaurants, orthodontics, cosmetics, and jewelry. Theoretically, she could claim the following combinations as her specialties:

Instructor	Restaurant procedures
	Department store sales
	Dental assisting
Hostess/Receptionist	Dental office
	Retail customer relations
Salesperson	Products broadly related to cosmetics and jewelry
	Math texts
	Orthodontic equipment and supplies
Supervisor	Department store sales
	Buying
Buyer	Products related to jewelry

These are all valid cross-linkings of functions with products/services, making an allowance for closely related products. Now Jennifer must choose the linkings that are not only the most practical but also the most compatible with her career objectives. She knows from her review of the accomplishments in which she takes the greatest pride (in other words, the things she likes to do and does best) that she should be in sales. Her ability to relate to customers and close orders is proven. She is attracted to field sales because of the potential for higher earnings and career advancement. She chooses as her new career targets:

- Sales of dental supplies and equipment
- Sales of fashion items to department stores

If needed, there is one other possibility lying in the weeds. Jennifer could fall back on her undergraduate minor in health care and combine that with her skill in sales to target field sales of health-care products or pharmaceuticals to retail outlets. But I suspect she will not have to.

Ralph Plans a Move

Ralph Miller is 45, married, and has three children, two of them still in college. He earned his B.A. from Drexel and his M.B.A. from Princeton. He is a certified public accountant. He golfs about twice a week, mostly with clients. He is an Elder in his church and teaches Bible study. He and his wife, Nancy, are active in a local theater workshop.

Ralph has been with Keystone Financial Services for fifteen years and has been a vice president for four. His specialty is recovery planning for sick businesses. He is assigned by his primary clients, banks and the like, to protect their investments by giving management assistance to floundering companies. Prior to Keystone, Ralph spent three years with the brokerage firm of Paine Webber and before that three years with the accounting firm of Arthur Young.

Ralph has never had to look for a job. Arthur Young hired him directly from his M.B.A. program on the strength of his 3.8 grade point average, and Paine Webber recruited him on the basis of a client's recommendation. Later the principal owner of Keystone, for whom Ralph handled investments, enticed him to join the staff. Now Keystone has been acquired through a stock deal, and Ralph is uneasy about the new owner, a Swiss company with a reputation for making sweeping management changes.

Ralph proceeds to compile his goal-setting lists:

Employment
Newspaper
Accounting firm

Brokerage house
Financial service company

Functions
Writer
Auditor
Broker of stocks and bonds
Business analyst and recovery planner
Manager

Products and Services
Wrote financial column for the local paper while in college
Specialized in auditing electronics and computer companies
Sold stocks in the electronics industry and related areas
Advised clients on individualized financial programs
Analyzed sick businesses and designed recovery plans
Managed recovery plans and trained new management

Accomplishments
Won the Brunswick award for an article covering Japanese business strategies
Brought about 35-percent increase in billing to assigned audit
customers by demonstrating to them the cost-effectiveness of
additional services; earned maximum bonus
Was placed in the top twenty brokers in the firm on the basis of
increased business
Earned a reputation for being the sick-company doctor through
planning and execution of recovery programs for companies
in or near bankruptcy

Ralph is proudest of his reputation for diagnosing the problems
of companies in trouble, producing a turnaround plan, and actually managing them back to health if necessary. This is what he
enjoys and does best.

After taking some time to reflect on the data in the four lists,
Ralph decides that he can choose either to continue his career in a
similar firm doing a similar job or to pursue the type of work he
enjoys by setting up his own consulting business. On further
thought, he adds two additional alternatives:

- General manager   Electronics manufacturing
- General manager   Computer-related industries

His experience as a sick-company doctor gives him valid managerial credentials.

Having gone through the goal-setting steps, Ralph now has a
plan on which he can base his campaign. Instead of wandering into
the job market in a random search for a job like the one he has, he

can set very specific targets. He knows where he is headed and why. Dumb luck might have brought him to the same point without all the advance planning, but I'd bet against it.

Work Worth Doing

If the efforts of Jennifer Rhodes and Ralph Miller strike you as more work than simply mailing out lots of standard resumes, you are correct. You were warned earlier that winning the new position of your choice would take work that only you could do. Using the tools and following the pathways will mean more effort initially, less in the long run, and a better job sooner. This holds true whether you are just beginning to think about a job change or are already active in the job market. Though in all fairness, I must admit to those who have no financial worries and need only to maintain the facade of looking for a job that a tally of many resumes mailed is a great cover. And just to be sure, they can flaunt a copy of this book.

The steps are simple, but they can be made unnecessarily complicated by such things as psychological evaluation and computerized self-analysis (further boons to the financially secure person who only wants to look like a diligent job seeker). However, one complication can be helpful: seeking out the opinion of a respected associate who knows your work. By discussing your new career targets with this person, you will get confirmation of your results and/or valuable new input. Choose this person with great care, being particularly careful not to choose someone who will tell you what he or she thinks you want to hear.

Diligently follow the goal-setting recipe: no shortcuts but plenty of thoughtful deliberation. You will then have great confidence about where you should aim your rifle.

Chapter 3

Tools and Pathways

"Your campaign for interviews and job offers does not have to be a struggle through uncharted jungle without a machete."

You are considering a new job. You get there by:

- Obtaining interviews with Decision Makers.
- Turning interviews into job offers.

Your campaign for interviews and job offers does not have to be a struggle through uncharted jungle without a machete. Tested tools are at hand and proven pathways here for the taking. They will lead you to DMs and to job offers.

Tools

First let's look at the four tools: networks, telephones, word processors, and resumes.

Networks

Networking, currently one of the most popular job-hunting buzzwords, means the process of contacting the people you know to tell them you are in the market for a job and encouraging them to pass the word to the people they know. The objective is to set into motion a team that will act as additional eyes and ears in support of your campaign. Advocates of networking claim that it leads to the "hidden job market," another buzzword that refers to those positions that are never advertised openly.

Networking can be very effective if done well. But there are three pitfalls. Networking, if overdone, can degenerate into a shotgun approach, waste valuable time, and add unwanted pounds.

Consider the case of Jennifer Rhodes, the buyer from Madison's Department Store whose situation we discussed in Chapter 2.

When Jennifer first began exploring the job market, she contacted people she knew. Among them was Jim, a former boss. Jim met Jennifer for lunch, only to report that he knew of no opening. But he wanted to help, so he referred her to his friend Jane. The results of a lunch with Jane were the same, but because any friend of Jim's was a friend of hers, Jane sent Jennifer on to Art.

Art had no position open and knew of none, but he did have a friend, so Jennifer was sent on her way to yet another lunch. At this point, she had invested about 6 hours going to, returning from, and participating in polite lunches, and the process could have gone on forever. All that was accomplished was that friends felt they had done favors for friends and Jennifer had gone off her diet. So use networking, by all means, but follow the friends and associates pathways as described in this chapter.

And remember this important piece of advice: avoid luncheon and dinner meetings. Restaurants are the worst place to be interviewed. The environment is not suitable for confidential discussion, there are constant distractions, and too much time is spent.

Telephones

It is highly unlikely that you will find your new career without using the telephone, but it is important to realize that the telephone is only a tool and not a pathway. Some experts suggest that a job search can be conducted almost entirely by phone; there is even a book on this technique. If you are a whiz at telemarketing and don't mind selling yourself by phone like oil stocks or precious metals, then this approach might work for you. Otherwise, keep in mind that the telephone is a means to an end and not an end in itself. Job hunting takes more than placing a few calls and waiting for a new job to arrive on your doorstep.

Word Processors

It is also highly unlikely that you will find your new job without communicating in writing. And because a focused approach to the target means greater success sooner, a standard letter and resume just won't do. You must have the ability to tailor your materials to fit the situation, taking into account both function and product. With word processing, this is as simple as punching a few keys.

Ninety-nine percent of the writing to support your job search will be typed. Notes of a personal nature and the rare letter can be handwritten, but do not expect to conduct a job campaign without typing capability. If you have a word processor, you're all set. If you don't have a word processor and you can type, buy or rent one. Otherwise, make sure you enlist the aid of someone skilled in word processing, whether a friend or professional secretarial help. You'll come to appreciate the efficiency and economy of word processing as you tailor your resumes, letters, and responses to help-wanted ads.

Resumes

As a first step, most job hunters mail out 100 copies of a freshly updated, all-purpose resume and wait for the flood of interview invitations that never comes. Chapter 4 discusses the art of resume writing in detail, offering the fruits of my hard-won wisdom. For now, remember that a resume, like a telephone, is a tool rather than a pathway, a means rather than an end.

Pathways

The six pathways to your new career are friends, associates, letters, job advertisements, recruiters, and employment applications. The first three are covered in this chapter, the last three in later chapters.

Friends

The best way to find a new job is through your friends. If you have thirty to forty years of experience, it may well be your only way, unless you are a Peter Ueberroth or Lee Iacocca. At the other end of the spectrum, entry level, friends are also especially important.

Whenever I have an opportunity to chat with people who have recently made a job change, I always ask how they found their new position, i.e., which pathway they followed. I estimate that 30 percent mention friends and another 20 percent cite associates. So you can see why I stress the prime importance of friends.

This is a good place to bring up "the age problem." If you have been around industry for forty years, you must be pushing sixty. Despite what the law says about age discrimination, you will certainly run into it as you approach senior-citizen status, and you might as well face the reality. A friend can help you sidestep the problem by giving you a job directly or by making a strong recommendation that scores for you. You will learn other helpful strategies in the course of this book.

At the other end of the spectrum, at entry level, a friend can lead you to a good place to work. When I had a choice early in my career, I picked General Electric because a long-time friend and GE employee bragged that it was a quality organization. He was right.

Don't forget, by the way, that there is no such thing as a confidential job search, even through friends. If your boss knows you are looking and gives you his blessing, fine. If there is no problem when he or she gets the news, fine again. However, if you are going to get fired when the news reaches the boss's desk, you had better have your new job firmly in hand. Run your job search as if the boss will soon find out about it, because, believe me, it will happen.

Your first effort in the job search should be to set up your network of friends. It is not simply a case of saying, "Hey, Joe, I need a job." In making your approach:

- Put it in writing.
- Make it clear that you are not asking for a job but only for additional eyes and ears to aid in your search.
- Describe the position you are looking for in terms of your function and product/service expertise.
- Remind your friend why you are qualified for the position you seek.
- Include a friendly note.

Jennifer Writes to a Friend

On the following page is an example of the kind of letter Jennifer Rhodes sent to her friends after she redirected her job search. This letter meets all the criteria. Jennifer assures Jill that she is not asking for a job. She mentions the position she is after and reminds Jill of her qualifications. Finally, there is a familiar note that reminds Jill of Jennifer's friendship, a subtle way of saying, "If I have earned any chips with you, I want to cash some of them in now."

A letter like this is not as easy to forget as a phone call or a conversation in the elevator. Jennifer's friend must either throw the letter in the trash or put it on her desk. If it ends up in the shredder, no harm done. If it sits on her desk, it stands a chance of getting some action.

Jill is now motivated and able to help. She is reminded of a friend in need, knows what to look for, and can comment on Jennifer's capability if and when an opportunity arises. Jennifer has added a valuable set of eyes and ears along this most important pathway to her new career.

Associates

The associates pathway, the second-best way to turn up a new job that matches your goals, is similar to the friends pathway, except that your letter must be more formal and more specific. Your mailing list is made up of people in your professional and civic life who will remember having worked with you. Pick people from among your customers, suppliers, and competitors, as well as from trade associations, civic committees, religious organizations, clubs, and seminars you have attended. Some discretion must be used in

Jennifer A. Rhodes
1111 Circle Drive
Los Angeles, CA 90027
213-555-3785

July 29, 1990

Dear Jill,

This note is just to let you know that I am in the job market. Madison's Department Store has been a good place to work, but I have gone as far as I can there. When we get together, I'll let you in on the details. Meanwhile, I just want you to know that I am looking.

Let me emphasize that I am not asking for a job at your company or for you to find one for me. I only want to alert you in case something comes to your attention that may be of interest.

My target is field sales of dental products, pharmaceuticals, or related lines. You will recall that I have been at Madison's for four years and have been a senior buyer in jewelry for the last two. I am proud to say that the products I selected were mainly responsible for the improved performance of the department.

My previous position was in retail sales of cosmetics and jewelry at Bronk's. Because of my sales record, I became the youngest sales supervisor in the nation for the Elson line of fine cosmetics. I got the job at Madison's because their jewelry department manager learned of my sales record through a sales rep. I did well in sales and was moved into buying with a substantial salary increase.

I earned my B.A. in business administration from the University of Vermont, with a minor in health care. I spent my first year out of school as a dental assistant. My objective is to combine the dental and health-care experiences with my skills in sales. My motivation is the potential for advancement and higher earnings.

Jill, I am not after a bunch of courtesy interviews over lunch. I can do without the calories, and I know other people have better things to do. However, if you do hear of anything that might be a fit, you know I will appreciate the help.

Give my best wishes to that great husband of yours. When this job thing is over, let's get together around my barbecue.

With best personal regards,

Jennifer

compiling the list, because contacting associates is the best way to announce your plans to the world. Approaching competitors will spread the news throughout your industry. If this tactic is not handled properly, it can backfire in various ways. If it looks at all like you are trying to sell your company's secrets, no one will touch you. You will have to read the circumstances carefully and make the political, professional, and ethical judgments necessary.

Jennifer Contacts a Business Associate

The letter to an associate should meet the same criteria as the letter to a friend, but replace the friendly note with a reminder of how you and the recipient know each other. On the following page is a sample letter, again from Jennifer Rhodes.

Mr. Godwin knows what Jennifer is after and why she is qualified. If he is so inclined, he will serve as useful eyes and ears for her, and, of course, there is always the possibility that he has a job for her.

The associates letter takes more effort than the friends letter, because you have to dig up the names and addresses and include the information that reminds the associate of how he or she knows you. But the effort is worth it, and with a word processor you can easily insert the information that identifies you in an otherwise standard letter.

Do not send your resume to either friends or associates. You cannot compose one resume that would fit the variety of opportunities that can occur along these pathways. If your friends and associates had a copy of your resume, they might very well send it to an interested Decision Maker. If that version of the resume was inappropriate to the situation, you would miss out on an opportunity. Without the resume, your friends and associates will call to alert you to job possibilities. Then you can take the time to research the companies in question and prepare targeted resumes.

Letters

This pathway is not unlike the broadcast letter technique discussed earlier, except that it substitutes a rifle for a shotgun. Each letter may take more effort than the all-purpose communications of the broadcast approach, but these letters are energy efficient: they pinpoint the target, and they get results.

To get a letter campaign going, pick a company, study it, and tailor your offensive accordingly. Picking companies is easy. You already know a number in your product/service specialty. Set your priorities. If they include staying in the same community, you'll restrict your efforts to local companies. If you run out of targets, your library will have a directory of companies in your area.

Jennifer A. Rhodes
1111 Circle Drive
Los Angeles, CA 90027
213-555-3785

July 29, 1990

Mr. Alfred B. Godwin
Marketing Manager
Edgemont Distributors, Inc.
2255 Harborview Drive
Oceanbay, CA 92654

Dear Mr. Godwin:

This is to let you know that I have decided to leave my position as senior buyer at Madison's. The job has been a good one but seems now to be a dead end. It has been a pleasure working with you and your staff. Together we made your Denzig line the most popular in the jewelry department.

I wanted you to know of my plans because in your sphere of influence you may come upon an opportunity that fits my background. Let me emphasize that I am not asking you for a job or for you to find one for me. I only want to alert you in case something comes to your attention that may be of interest. My target is field sales of dental products, pharmaceuticals, or related lines.

You will recall that I have been at Madison's for four years and have been a senior buyer in jewelry for the last two. I am proud to say that the products I selected were mainly responsible for the improved performance of the department. My previous position was in retail sales of cosmetics and jewelry at Bronk's. Because of my sales record, I became the youngest sales supervisor in the nation for the Elson line of fine cosmetics. I won the job at Madison's because their jewelry department manager learned of my sales record through one of your sales reps. I did well in sales and was moved into buying with a substantial salary increase.

I earned my B.A. in business administration from the University of Vermont, with a minor in health care. I spent my first year out of school as a dental assistant. My objective is to combine the dental and health-care experiences with my skills in sales. My motivation is the potential for advancement and higher earnings.

Mr. Godwin, I am not after courtesy interviews. I know people have better things to do. However, if you do hear of anything that might be a fit, you know I will appreciate the help.

Sincerely,
Jennifer A. Rhodes

The information in a typical directory includes products, sales volume, number of employees, and key management names for the companies listed. For example, *The Florida Industries Guide* (Industries Guides, Inc., Orlando) and *Directory of Florida Industries* (Florida Chamber of Commerce, Coral Gables) are annuals that can be purchased for less than $50. The first one lists companies by city, the second by county. Other states and regions are covered by similar publications. Depending on the extent of your search, you may find it convenient and worth the investment to own your own copy of a directory. A word of caution: the criterion for inclusion in such a directory seems to be only that a company return a questionnaire, so some companies are bound to be missing.

If your search has no geographic restrictions, you have a wide choice of information sources. One of the most useful is *Million Dollar Directory* (Dun & Bradstreet, Parsippany, N.J.). Your library will have a copy, or the directory can be leased from the publisher. This volume lists all the organizations in the U.S. with a net worth of around $2-million or more. Companion volumes include smaller companies with a net worth of over $500,000. Your library may have these, too.

Each of the companies in these directories is listed with its Standard Industrial Code, the so-called SIC code. The government assigns an SIC code to every line of business and product. The first two digits of the code represent a major industry, the third digit represents a subgroup within that industry, and the fourth specifies the exact product or service a company deals in. This makes it very handy for job seekers to pick targets. Suppose, for example, that you are a specialist in Irish potatoes. The SIC alphabetical index in *Million Dollar Directory* tells you that the code for this product is 0134. You want to live in Rocky Mount, Virginia, so you turn to the index that lists SIC codes by state and city. There you find that your chosen town is big in 2499, 2436, 2269, and 2452, but not 0134. You are not going to blossom in Rocky Mount, at least not in potatoes. You will have to switch to wood products, soft wood veneers, the finishing of textiles, or prefabricated wood buildings to make your way in Rocky Mount.

On the other hand, if you decide to stay with potatoes and forgo the pleasures of Virginia, you simply go to the numerical index of SIC codes. There you will find that there are some thirty companies that dig Irish potatoes, listed by location—among them Bakersfield, California; Aberdeen, Idaho; Hoople, North Dakota; and Plover, Wisconsin. Through this handy system of classification, the Irish potato world is laid at your feet by our friends in the government.

A Letter Campaign for John

Consider the case of John Allard, who has decided to venture into the job market. He has been married to Nancy, his second wife, for twelve years. They have two children, a boy of 11 and a girl of 7, and they own their home in Brockton, Massachusetts.

John is 38 years old and holds a B.A. and an M.A. in education from Boston College. While studying for his M.A., John taught high school math and science in the Boston school system for four years. When approached through a fellow member of the Toastmasters Club, John joined the corporate communications staff of Logan Laboratories. He liked teaching but was attracted by the much higher income this position offered. He advanced to become director of communications reporting to the executive vice president, in which capacity he had responsibility for employee, stockholder, and financial-community communications.

After eight years with Logan, John ventured out on his own as a consultant, specializing in the same areas of communications. He expanded his business to include a professional staff of eight and achieved moderate success in terms of revenue and profit. But the hassle of 60-hour weeks, in which he handled personally all the details of the operation, and the stacks of government paperwork required of a small business drove him to the conclusion that he was not the type to be an entrepreneur for life. He has decided to look for a salaried position where the pressures are less great and where he will be able to spend more time with his family. Nancy firmly supports his decision, even if it means less income.

John Allard arrives at his objectives through the goal-setting process, listing his employment, functions, products/services, and accomplishments. Here is a summary of his data:

Employment
Handyman Hardware
Boston College
Boston school system
Logan Laboratories
Allard & Associates

Functions
Stock boy
Campus police deputy
Teacher
Communications specialist
Employee relations
Stockholder and financial-community relations

Consultant
Business manager

Products and Services
General hardware
Campus security patrol
Chemistry, physics, mathematics
Scientific measurement and analysis equipment
Industrial controls
Computer peripherals

Accomplishments
Revised inventory and stocking procedures to reduce outages and back orders; received a week's pay as a bonus
Students consistently exceeded test grade averages of the school system
Established communications programs that were credited in large part with convincing employees that a union was not needed
Won three honorable mentions for annual reports prepared for clients
Conducted my own business for over five years and had reasonable success

John considers aiming for a general management post in the communications business on the basis of his experience running his own business. (As has been said, "Find an individual who has started a business and survived, and you have one who is a leader or a manager, and most likely both.") However, he feels that a general manager's job would involve him in much the same strife he is trying to leave behind, only he would be doing it for someone else. And he is not sure others will consider him qualified as a general manager, since he is not walking away from his company a millionaire.

After reviewing his accomplishments, John decides he wants to concentrate on what he likes to do best: creating effective communications programs for management, employees, investors, and stockholders. The target he sets for his new-job campaign is communications specialist.

Since he owns his own business, John does not have a "drop dead date," a deadline by which he has to have a new job in hand. There is no boss to find out that John is looking. And John will, of course, tell clients of his intention so they won't hear it through the rumor circuit. John has the friends and associates parts of his campaign well under way and is into the letters phase. The Boston area is his primary geographic target, and since he and Nancy have often thought about living in the Seattle area, that becomes a secondary target.

The *Million Dollar Directory* tells John that the correct SIC codes are 7392 (consulting and public relations services) and 4899 (communication management). The same source describes the companies in Massachusetts and the Seattle area that fall under these codes. One of those John pinpoints appears as follows:

MC GRAW COMMUNICATIONS, INC.
2001 114th Ave NE, Seattle, WA

Zip 98003	*Tel* (206) 555-1911
Sales 25MM	*Emp* 350

SIC 4899 7392 Communication Management, Consulting and Public Relations Services

Robert Elton	*Ch Bd*
Thomas Finn	*Pr*
Darlene Scott	*VP*
Judith Prince	*VP*

From this listing, John can begin to gather the information he needs to tailor his letter approach. He can aim a rifle rather than a shotgun. The number of employees in the company indicates that McGraw could have a sizable creative department.

On the following pages are John's letter to McGraw Communications and his resume. The letter is right on course. It is directed to a Decision Maker: Mr. Elton is chairman of the board. It is brief and to the point. Its purpose is clear. If Mr. Elton needs a communications specialist, he will talk to Allard. If he doesn't, neither this nor any other letter will create the need.

By now you're probably saying to yourself, "Aha! A resume at last!" But don't fret. The finer points of this resume and resume writing in general will be discussed in the following chapter. It is sufficient to point out here that John's resume illustrates all the elements that make a mailing a rifle shot. The objective is clearly stated. Mr. Elton will know precisely what John is after. There is no doubt as to where Allard's skills lie or that they tie in with the interests of McGraw Communications.

Both letter and resume are a single page, yet they give Mr. Elton all the information he needs. If he is considering adding a communications specialist to his company, he will interview John Allard. If he isn't, the letter will end up in a file, round or rectangular, with no harm done. Allard will go on to another target. The effort cost some time and a stamp, but if you find out how to land a new job without the expenditure of either, please let me know and you can write the next book!

John R. Allard
33 Elm Street
Brockton, MA 02403
617-555-6345

July 23, 1990

Mr. Robert Elton
Chairman of the Board
McGraw Communications, Inc.
2001 114th Avenue NE
Seattle, WA 98003

Dear Mr. Elton:

In the event that you can use an additional Communications Specialist in your company, please consider my qualifications.

I am in the process of selling Allard & Associates, the communications company that I started five years ago. The business grew to eight employees and had annual sales of $775,000 and a reputation for excellence. However, I have learned that I am more suited to creative endeavors than to managing a small company.

Mr. Elton, perhaps I can prove useful to your company. A resume is enclosed. I will follow up with a call.

Sincerely,

John R. Allard

JRA/sef
Enclosure

RESUME

John R. Allard
33 Elm Street
Brockton, MA 02403
617-555-6345

OBJECTIVE
To contribute to the profitable growth of a company by applying my creative skills in the fields of employee, stockholder, and financial-community communications.

EDUCATION
B.A. with a major in education, Boston College, 1973
M.A. in education, Boston College, 1976

EMPLOYMENT
1985–Present: Owner, Allard & Associates, Boston

Providing clients with integrated communications programs for employees, stockholders, and the financial community. Company has grown to annual revenues of over $750,000. Product specialties include computers, computer peripherals, industrial controls, etc. For three years running, company has won honorable mention for annual reports in competition with over 3,000 entries.

1977–1985: Director of Communications, Logan Laboratories, Boston

Managed the company's employee relations, stockholder, and financial-community communications programs. Created and implemented information program that was credited with convincing employees there was no need for a union. Logan's annual reports were consistently rated among the best in the industry. At my instigation, four articles featuring the Laboratories were written by financial analysts.

1973–1977: Teacher of Mathematics and Science, Boston School System

My students consistently received higher grades than other students.

PERSONAL
Married, two children
Born 7/29/51

Chapter 4

Resumes

"There is absolutely no room for humility in a resume."

Resumes come in an almost infinite variety. A few are excellent; the great majority are mediocre. Resume writing is the aspect of job search where a lack of expertise is most apparent. I have reviewed thousands of resumes in my executive search work, and this experience, coupled with what I have gained through my own job campaigns, has led me to formulate nine rules that will make a resume stand out.

Resume Rule 1
Specialize Each Resume to Each Target

You will have no use in your job search for a "standard resume." Get hold of a word processor and target each resume to meet a specific job or career objective. Remember how John Allard highlighted certain aspects of his background in the resume he prepared for Mr. Elton at McGraw Communications.

At first you may not place much importance on this rule, but you will come to appreciate that a little effort put into making your resumes fit specific objectives will produce many more interviews than will the production of one all-purpose resume. This becomes even more critical as your urgency factor increases or your career level advances.

Resume Rule 2
Keep the Resume to One Page

I predict that you will have greater difficulty complying with this rule than with any of the others. Most of us are convinced that more is better. But as we will see in Chapter 5, which discusses the hiring process, a resume should provide only what's necessary to reach the immediate goal—an interview—and nothing more.

I have a file I call "Bad Resumes" where I keep the worst offenders I've encountered over the years. The winner in the "most voluminous" category came from Mr. I. Gush, who presented twelve pages of irrelevant information in a plastic cover. Just a few of the things he listed were his informal education, with subheadings for readings and practical experience, and ten separate items under each; nineteen seminars and courses he had attended; five social memberships, including a country club; thirteen magazines he read regularly, including *Playboy;* ten sports and hobbies he participated in, including dancing; and, finally, his height and weight.

Incidentally, this person was competing with over 100 candidates for a position as vice president. Perhaps he thought the very bulk of his resume would make him unforgettable. He did not get the job. I did.

Make every word count, and you can easily fit the important information on one page. If you must list publications, patents, and awards, keep the list to one page and attach it as an appendix.

Resume Rule 3

Include a Company-Oriented Statement of Objective

Your statement of objective should be an attention-getter. It should be concise and aimed at the target. Rambling at this point may lose your audience, so get your point across quickly. State the job you want and how you can help the company.

Hundreds of resumes cross my desk each year. It takes just a second or two for me to decide whether I'm interested or not. If I took the time to read every word of every resume, I wouldn't have any time to work for my clients. So remember, when your resume arrives on the desk of a busy Decision Maker, he or she has better things to do than labor over it trying to dig out the pertinent information.

Consider doctors, who have many anxious patients waiting to see them. "Detailers," the people who sell products to doctors, must compete with patients for the doctor's time. The fact that the doctor can't bill the detailer for time spent in the office makes the competition even tougher. The salesperson is taught to start selling as soon as he or she has the doctor's attention. One product is presented as the detailer walks into the office, another at the desk, and a third on the way out. These salespeople are efficient—they tell their story simply and quickly. Picture your resume passing before a busy Decision Maker and you will see that it needs to be sold in the same way. Start with an effective and realistic statement of objective and include only the most pertinent data in your resume.

What makes for an effective statement of objective? I selected 100 resumes at random from my files. Forty-four of them had no statement of objective. Thirty-four had statements too egotistical to be helpful. Seventeen simply listed job titles. Only five of them had a statement of objective that was written with the company in mind.

In effect, the resumes with no statement of objective were asking the Decision Maker to figure out where the candidate fit in. This just doesn't work in today's job market.

The egotistical statements either declared what the candidates wanted the company to do for them, bragged, or did both. For example:

> "Position as an attorney with emphasis on general corporate and securities law. My ideal job would be with a law department that provides advancement potential, rewards for individual initiative, and a mix of general corporate law, corporate financing, and securities matters."

Any DM would be justified in asking what the company was going to get in return for providing the ideal job for this candidate. Here's another example:

> "MULTIFACETED EXECUTIVE HAVING DIVERSIFIED EXPERIENCE/EDUCATION IN BOTH THE PUBLIC AND PRIVATE SECTORS, WITH STRENGTHS IN MARKETING, FINANCE, AND SALES. LOOKING FOR A POSITION THAT OFFERS GROWTH AND CAREER OPPORTUNITY IN A PROGRESSIVE COMPANY."

Not only did this candidate brag and tell the company what it could do for him, but he put it all in capital letters! And one last sample:

> "An administrative position where interpersonal skills and creative ability can be fully utilized."

This one is not as flagrantly full of ego, but the candidate's main concern is still to be "fully utilized" rather than to do something for the company.

Simply stating a job title is not a bad way to go. Here are some examples from the seventeen that took this approach:

Comptroller	Auditor
Project or Design Engineer	Interior Decorator
Senior Marketing Manager	Loan Officer
International Sales Manager	Property Appraiser
Plant Engineer	Apartment Manager

But to make your resume one of the 5 percent that truly stand out, include a statement of objective that is clear, concise, and company oriented. Here are the five winners in my sample of 100:

> "A challenging career position with a highly reputable organization where my education, experience, and abilities in the areas of sales, management, and finance would be of value."

> "To contribute to the development of diagnostic tools and test procedures for computer systems and peripherals."

> "To serve as Regional Director of Security/Loss Prevention for a retail chain, providing security leadership and professional investigative techniques to reduce internal and external loss."

> "A responsible position in Corporate Finance where sixteen years of diversified experience managing financial functions and systems will contribute to the organization's management style, productivity, and profit growth."

> "To be an efficient and effective Buyer or Purchasing Agent, procuring products for the increased productivity of the company."

The last one is the overall winner. The writer left no doubt about what she wanted to do or that it would be done for the benefit of the company. (The first is too general, but at least the writer wanted to "be of value" to the company.)

In the real world of job search, Decision Makers want to know what you are going to do for them. When you win a position, you will soon be told that the company provides growth opportunity, sound management, excellent benefits, an attractive working environment, etc. However, the decision to offer you the job will be based on what you can do for the company and not on what the company can do for you. You will be reminded often of this basic tenet of the job search as we proceed, but the first place to apply it is in writing the statement of objective on your resume. State the job you want and *how you will help the company*.

Resume Rule 4
Include Accomplishments

An early mentor of mine once said, "It matters not where you have been, only what you have accomplished." Nowhere is this truer than in resume writing. "Obvious!" you say. Not so obvious. Here is an all-too-typical extract from a resume I received:

SUMMARY OF BUSINESS EXPERIENCE
City Manager for a city with a population of 28,000
- Administered personnel policies
- Provided for public safety
- Supervised public works
- Directed city planning
- Arranged for community services
- Provided health services
- Prepared and administered the budget
- Managed technical services

These words tell nothing of what the person has *accomplished*. They simply describe areas of exposure. When I encounter experiences without accomplishments, I have the urge to write in the margin, "and screwed up so badly had to find another job."

Perhaps it is the puritan ethic that causes us to downplay our achievements. But there is absolutely no room for humility in a resume. Fight it with the philosophy attributed to Yogi Berra: "It ain't bragging if it's true." Save your modesty for handling the congratulations when you win the job.

Lynn Longmyer Applies the Rules

Lynn Longmyer wants to reenter the job market. She is married, 38 years old, and has two young children, a girl of 5 and a boy of 3. Her husband of ten years is manager of passenger services for an airline that transferred him to Atlanta. The family moved there a year ago.

After high school, Lynn earned an A.A. degree from the Olentangy School of Design in Columbus, Ohio, and then spent four years working for a local advertising agency, first in the graphics department and then as a copywriter. From there she was recruited as an account executive by a larger agency. When she left eight years later to start a family, she had become manager of the graphics department and supervised a staff of sixteen. Lynn has freelanced in graphics and copy writing since moving to Atlanta but now wants to reestablish a full-time career. Since she left most of her contacts in Ohio, she must establish new ones for her job campaign. Following the procedures described earlier, Lynn breaks down her job history like this:

Employment
Charley's Steak House
Boutique Freda

The Drake Fry Agency
Eric Hamilton & Associates
Numerous small firms as a free-lancer

Functions
Waitress
Retail clerk
Graphic designer
Copywriter
Account executive
Department manager

Products and Services
Lunch and dinner
Women's apparel
Ad layouts and copy
Advertising programs
Advertising sales, program management, customer service
Departmental responsibilities: budgeting, scheduling, personnel, etc.

Accomplishments
Promoted to sales supervisor at the boutique while still a student in design school
Graduated second in class at design school
My design won a contest to provide client with a new logo
Created ad campaign that resulted in $200,000-worth of new business for the agency
Recruited two top designers for the company
Received a management award as graphics department manager

Lynn has been successful in graphics, copy writing, and management, facts borne out by her accomplishments. She has successfully managed a departmental staff and has been recognized for her skills in graphics and copy writing. However, having been away from the routine of regular employment for several years now, Lynn realizes that she will not be able to pick up where she left off but will likely have to take a position that enables her to come back up to speed.

After reviewing her goal-setting process and evaluating her accomplishments, Lynn sees that what she liked best and did well at was her job as account executive. She enjoyed the mix of customer-service and technical skills the job required. This, then, becomes her goal. Being realistic, Lynn doesn't expect a company to put her in charge of a customer account right away. But she does expect to be given a shot at working her way up from a junior position and so decides to aim for a job in customer service with an ad agency. This job would involve responding to customer's inquiries, preparing status reports, administering changes—tasks that would highlight her customer-service and technical skills. Lynn prepared the resume on the next page in support of her campaign for a customer-service position with an ad agency.

This resume shows that Lynn Longmyer did more than just appear on the scene. It lists some of her accomplishments. It will help set her apart from other candidates. It will help her win the job she wants. Notice that Lynn does not go into detail on the resume about her four years as a full-time homemaker. She wisely leaves it for the interviewer to ask her about those years when the time comes.

Resume Rule 5
Never State Salary Requirements

Coming to an agreement on compensation is a key facet of your campaign (see Chapter 17), but the resume is no place to start negotiating. You will either leave money on the table or eliminate yourself before you've even had an interview. Even when you're responding to an ad that instructs you to include your salary history or requirements, don't. As we discuss in the next chapter, you won't be eliminated for this omission if you play your cards right. (The one exception to Rule 5 occurs when you are writing a resume for a search firm. This is explained in Chapter 6.)

Resume Rule 6
Indicate Your Age

In spite of all the rhetoric about how age should never be considered in hiring, in the real world age is an important factor. It is primarily a concern for older candidates, but the young are also affected when their skills outrun their years.

Some job seekers try to hide their age, and others simply lie about it. The hiders leave the information off their resume and hope nobody will notice. The liars give false data, dye their hair, and worry about being caught. They always are, of course, if not before reporting for work, then very soon thereafter. Hardly an ideal way to start a new job.

Your resume must allude to your age, or it will appear that there is a problem. If you are young—say, under fifty—add your date of birth to the resume. If you are pushing the half-century mark, you should consider softening the age presentation. It depends on the position you are after. When nearing sixty, you definitely want to

RESUME

Lynn A. Longmyer
3354 Peachtree Circle
Atlanta, GA 30314
404-555-3961

OBJECTIVE
To obtain a position in Customer Service with an advertising agency where my fifteen years of experience will contribute to growth and profitability.

EMPLOYMENT
Free-lance Advertising, 1988–Present

Providing ad graphics and copy for local agencies and clients. Products and services include auto repair, computer sales, home building, and personnel services. The campaign created for Edmont Homes was cited as the "season's best" by the Association of Builders and Developers.

On sabbatical, 1983–1987

Eric Hamilton & Associates, 1975–1983

Hired as an Account Executive. Created and implemented programs for clients. Won three "readership awards": *Better Homes and Gardens, Woman's World,* and *Country Decorating.* Brought a $200,000-a-year client into the company by designing and selling a new program in competition with three biggest agencies in the area.

   Promoted to Manager of Graphics. Established new standards of excellence by motivating existing staff and recruiting two top designers. Received a special bonus for department performance in 1983.

Drake Fry Agency, 1971–1975

Worked in both graphics and copy writing. Trained by Gene Worth, an influential leader in the industry. Created the design that won a client's new logo contest.

EDUCATION
A.A. degree with a concentration in graphic arts, 1971, Olentangy School of Design, Columbus, Ohio.

ease the blow. You do this by letting the Decision Maker calculate your age from your education data. For example:

Graduate, Pembroke High, 1946
B.A. with a major in business administration, UCLA, 1952

This enables the Decision Maker to do some math and approximate your age. This approach is neither clever nor subtle, but it does take the edge off an outright announcement of approaching senior citizenship.

Again, in the case of a resume to a recruiter, you must hang all the years out there without camouflage. Some recruiters are actually as old as you and I and will know the value of maturity, wisdom, practicality, and intelligence—the qualities that come automatically with senior citizenship.

Chapter 19 takes a more detailed look at the issues facing the mature job candidate.

Resume Rule 7

Put Pertinent Education Data Up Front

Your education is important only in relation to the goal you are pursuing. If you are looking for a position as a science teacher, highlight your B.S. with a major in physics. But if you're hot to become a commodities broker, your degree in physics deserves only casual mention. It might even be a detriment: a prospective employer might ask if your physics training was relevant to commodities or whether you wouldn't get bored after a while and want to go back to physics.

John Allard in Chapter 3 was after a position in corporate communications. His education was strong and relevant to the job, so he featured it up front on his resume. Lynn Longmyer's A.A. with a concentration in graphic arts was relevant to her job search but not as strong as if it were a B.A. She could have gone either way but chose to list education last.

Resume Rule 8

Avoid the Job-Hopper Image

Nothing gives a worse impression than a rolling-stone resume: a rapid-fire list of many jobs held over a short span of years. Once again, I suspect this results from some conviction that more is better and honesty is the best policy.

Frank Torez Tells All

Consider part of Frank Torez's resume on the next page. He was after a marketing job in the chemical polymer industry. Do not get

RESUME

Frank P. Torez
1875 Walnut Avenue
San Rafael, CA 94912
415-555-4567

PROFESSIONAL EXPERIENCE
January 1986–Present: Director of R&D and Marketing, Polytech, Inc., Dublin, California
Managed the development and marketing of structural components from continuous prepreg, both thermoset and thermoplastic, using glass, graphite, epoxies, polyimides, etc.

March 1983–December 1985: Marketing Manager for Polymers, Chemrem, Inc., Walnut Ridge, California
Managed and implemented R&D of polyimide foams, adhesives, and laminating resin technology and directed marketing of products.

January 1982–March 1983: Sales Manager, Acme Specialties, Inc., Walnut Ridge, California
Responsible for sales of all products, including new polymers and structural materials for aerospace. New polymers included special formulations for high-temperature applications. Structures were for leading-edge and other severe-environment applications.

May 1981–January 1982: Business Manager, Aerospace Products, Y & Z Chemical Co., Irvine, California
Position encompassed profit responsibility for aerospace structural products using glass and graphite prepregs with epoxies and polyimides.

January 1980–May 1981: New Product Manager, W. S. Richter, Inc., Dublin, California
Coordinated all new-product development for three domestic divisions. Products included plastic seals and ball bearings.

January 1976–January 1980: General Manager, Fantatech Corp., Irvine, California
Compounding and molding of engineering thermosets and thermoplastics: polyesters, epoxies, polyimides. As General Manager, was also Technical Director.

March 1974–January 1976: Marketing Specialist, Ryan-Levin, Inc., San Rafael, California
Sold polyimide molding and laminating resins to the electronics industry.

hung up on the descriptions of each job; do pay attention to the dates of employment for each position.

It went on like this, all the way back to 1969. This candidate had held eight jobs in twenty years and bragged about it. This is an average of two and a half years at each position. Not many Decision Makers will want to interview a candidate who is likely to move on in another two years. Just the time and money invested in recruiting make him an unattractive choice, regardless of his qualifications. This candidate is stuck with his employment history, but he is not obliged to advertise it.

Remember, *the purpose of a resume is to help get an interview.* This one shouts "rolling stone," which is enough to send it to the shredder and leave Frank adrift in the job market. And there were other problems. For the purposes of this discussion, I abbreviated the job descriptions and left out the education information and list of publications and patents. The original treatise covered five pages, but even at that it did not contain any accomplishments. There was no statement of objective.

A presentation like this would have to be extensively revised to be of any help in winning an interview. Gaining an interview will not solve the rolling-stone problem, but it will give you an opportunity to overcome it in person by stressing your strong points and explaining how you will help the company. There are no rules that say you must tell all.

It is possible for Torez to relate his background and experience without highlighting the fact that he has not stayed at one job for any length of time. Departing from reverse chronological order and describing functional and product/service experience can accomplish this. On the following page is a revised resume for Frank Torez that illustrates this approach. Notice that education is relevant and has been put in a prominent position. Following the resume is the appendix, in which Frank's pertinent publications and patents are listed. A note on the resume refers the reader to the appendix.

The Torez case demonstrates how a poorly written resume can limit the chances of a good candidate. Frank was very well qualified to move up in a fast-growing industry. His education was good, his experience relevant, and his accomplishments significant. If I were presenting Frank to a client, I would send him off with the improved version of his resume and, once he got an interview, coach him to discuss openly the number of jobs he has held. At the interview, he would have a chance to sell himself by acknowledging his many jobs and then highlighting his strengths.

RESUME

Frank P. Torez
1875 Walnut Avenue
San Rafael, CA 94912
415-555-4567

OBJECTIVE

To obtain a position in Marketing where my background and experience in advanced polymeric resins and advanced composite structures will contribute to growth and profitability.

EDUCATION

B.S. Plastics Engineering, Rensselaer Polytechnic Institute, 1968

EXPERIENCE

Since graduation, have specialized in the research, development, and marketing of products derived from polymer chemistry, including polyesters, epoxies, and polyimides. Expertise includes thermoset and thermoplastic systems, glass, and graphite. End products were resins, adhesives, prepregs, and fabricated components. Background includes:

Director of R&D and Marketing, Polytech, Inc., Dublin, California
Management of new thermoplastic product development and marketing. Company's principal products are continuous prepreg for aerospace structures. In three years, developed backlog of $10-million in new markets. Developed and qualified the 7893 Matrix System for the Advanced Astronomical Platform in less than two years.

Marketing Manager for Polymers, Chemrem, Inc., Walnut Ridge, California
Developed polyimide structural foams and adhesives for Air Force and NASA applications. Obtained $13-million contract for the critical-heat protective application for the Espy Mission by formulating and qualifying an advanced resin system. Obtained the company's first large Air Force contract by adapting System 197 to the new syntactic specification before the competition could react.

General Manager, Fantatech Corp., Irvine, California
Company's products were advanced engineered plastics, both thermoset and thermoplastic. Started the company as Torez Industries and grew it to $2.5-million annual sales in three years selling to aerospace markets. Sold the company to Fantatech and remained as General Manager with responsibility for P&L and R&D. Grew the company to annual sales of $5.5-million in four years.

PUBLICATIONS AND PATENTS

Have published nine articles in the field and have been issued two patents for advanced polymer formulations. See enclosed appendix.

PERSONAL

Born 9/29/46; married, three children

APPENDIX
Frank P. Torez Resume

PUBLICATIONS
"Bearings Without Lubrication." *Plastic Innovations,* 1972.

"Polyimides Applied to Molding Compounds." *Plastic Engineering,* 1974.

"Polyimides for High-Temperature Applications." *Society of Plastic Engineering,* 1978.

"Reinforced Polymeric Alloys." *SAPP,* 1980.

"High-Performance Polyblends." *SPEE,* 1981.

"650°F Thermoplastics." *SAPP,* 1985.

"Trends in High-Temperature Polymerization." *ACSC,* 1986.

PATENTS
Polymerization of Polyphenylene, 1977.
Polyimide Polyalloy, 1983.

If you have been around a while and have held several positions, how many and which should you list? There is no single answer to this question. It depends on the situation. However, it's probably a good idea to hold it down to five, picking the most appropriate ones for your particular target.

A note of caution: in their desire to tell all, some candidates will give the appearance of being job hoppers by listing all the positions they have held within one company, including the dates for each. Someone taking a quick glance at an arrangement of this sort gets

47

the impression of a "rolling stone," even if this is not the case. Most resumes get little more than a quick glance to begin with, so avoid this unnecessary pitfall. Describe all your experiences at a particular company under a single set of dates.

Resume Rule to End All Resume Rules
Omit Superfluous Information

All sorts of other stuff can be thrown into a resume—and most of it has been. So I'll remind you again that the *only* purpose of a resume is to help you get an interview. Everything in the resume must contribute to this end. Anything that does not is not only wasted but possibly detrimental.

By all means, if you're bilingual or multilingual, say so. This is an asset. It's nice to mention that you're married, but don't take the space away from your specialties and accomplishments to do so. And you can leave out "references provided upon request," "excellent health," "will travel," and "will relocate."

As already mentioned, patents and publications should be listed in an appendix. However, make sure they are relevant to your target. If you want to be regional manager for a retail chain, mention your article "Swimwear Trends of the Baby-Boom Male" but leave out "Bird-Watching Along the Amazon."

Given the present interpretation of the personal liability laws, references have lost a lot of their meaning. The exception is the case in which someone is after your scalp. If someone is out to get you, he or she will find a way to be negative within the law. Later you will learn how to handle this kind of situation. But the typical person, when called, will refer the reference-checker to the personnel department, where the caller will be given employment dates, salary, and nothing more (and maybe not even that).

No need to volunteer information about the state of your health. The DM will know all about it after the pre-employment physical that is routine at many companies today.

As to commenting that you will travel, don't bother. In the current business environment, anyone not willing to travel should join a monastery. (But choose carefully or you may end up in Zanzimbie.)

When your goal is a job with an out-of-town company, stating that you will relocate is, of course, superfluous. It might be helpful to know that you'd move if the company you approached in Trenton, New Jersey, was looking for someone in their East Moccasin, Nebraska, office, but, in any event, why not let them ask?

As a service to those who don't really want a job but need to present a convincing facade of looking for one, here are some things to do with a resume to ensure that you won't be harassed by anything so inconvenient as an interview or a job offer.

Include your picture. When the DM reads the information presented in your resume, he or she may form a mental picture of you, like it, and decide to interview you. But when the page is turned and that mental image is replaced by a photographic one, the Decision Maker may very well have a change of heart. The DM's mental image will beat your glossy anytime.

Include letters of recommendation. If you don't have any, get Aunt Hattie to write a few.

Take a lead from our friend with the ten-page dissertation enclosed in plastic covers, and pack your resume with enough material to justify a table of contents and an index.

Print it on flashy paper so it will *really* stand out.

Use the same version for everyone you send it to.

List all your memberships—Elks, Knights of Columbus, Masons, Daughters of the American Revolution, etc. You are bound to put off some of the Decision Makers.

Mention your politics. Republican or Democrat or Socialist, you stand a good chance of offending at least half of the DMs and maybe all of them.

List your high-risk sports: hang gliding, scuba diving, drag racing, lion taming, skydiving. You'll be ruled out by those narrow-minded managers who dislike hiring someone with a death wish.

List everything you have ever done: staff management, personnel management, motor-pool management, cafeteria management, copy-machine management, paper-clip management . . . you get the idea.

If you want to make a career out of this phase of the job hunt, there are a number of books about resumes. The typical bookstore carries at least six such works that contain enough material to keep you reading for days. I've even found one called *How to Rewrite Your Resume,* which is presumably based on the assumption that after you've used all the other resume books, you're going to need just this one more. Browse through these books and their theoretical advice on typing format, action adverbs and adjectives, size of type, etc. You will soon return to the practical advice of this chapter. However, if you choose to dwell on the trivia of preparing a resume rather than get on with your job search, you can even buy a computer program for writing resumes. It will cost you about $50 and should keep you off the job market for at least two weeks while you play with it.

Before we leave this chapter, let's revisit our resume rules by looking at the revised Torez resume.

- It is specialized to hit its target.
- It is one page long.
- It includes a statement of objective that is company oriented.
- It lists accomplishments.
- It does not mention salary requirements.
- It states the applicant's age clearly.
- It mentions relevant education near the top.
- It avoids the job-hopping problem.
- It contains no superfluous information.

Remember these points. You now have all you need to write the kind of resume that will help you get interviews.

Chapter 5

Answering Want Ads

"You can win an interview through any ad. The challenge is to be able to get the job offer once you are onstage."

The following ad appeared recently in the *Wall Street Journal* (it has been paraphrased slightly, as have all the ads in this chapter):

PRESIDENT

- Are you a leader? Can you get results?
- Do you establish positive relationships?
- Can you bring out the best in people?
- Do you thrive in a fast-moving company?
- Are you a good communicator?
- Do you consider manufacturing a "people business"?

If the answers are "yes," you may be the one for this opportunity of a lifetime. We are a progressive manufacturer in the home appliance industry.

WE OFFER

- Excellent salary
- Performance bonus
- A chance to express your creativity

If your background includes operations and marketing in a manufacturing environment as a Senior Officer, and if you are ready for your last career change . . . Call now!

Dr. Paul Hartung or Mildred Beauchamp
800-555-5693

This job advertisement drew 961 responses. From these, three were selected for an interview. Here's another one:

VENTURE CAPITAL   Major New York–based Venture Capital organization is seeking two outstanding individuals to join the firm as Associates. Job functions will be to evaluate investment proposals, make investment recommendations, and work with portfolio companies.

Ideal candidates will have superior analytical and communications skills, as well as two to six years of experience. Technical and M.B.A. degrees preferred. Write to Box LL-349, the WSJ.

There were over 900 responses to this national advertisement. This next one drew 450 replies:

SALES VICE PRESIDENT

Outstanding opportunity to spearhead U.S. corporate sales for a publicly held company. Become a member of a proven management team selling high-tech products and services that maximize corporate productivity. Requires top-level sales success and management experience. This unique opportunity offers personal achievement and capital gain. Please send resume and earnings history in confidence to:

Search Committee, BOTTOM LINE PRODUCTS, INC.
50 North Wacker Drive, Chicago, IL 60606

The president of this company invited forty prospects to New York for a personal interview. I was one of them, but when I asked to be reimbursed for my expenses, my request was denied and I was removed from the contention. Herein lies a lesson: establish up front who pays for the interview trip. Leave no doubt. When you are invited to attend an interview, simply say, "I am willing to invest my time if you are willing to cover the travel and living expenses." If the company is not willing, forget it.

Forty is an unusually large number of interviewees, a tip-off that something fishy was going on. This impression was confirmed when the same ad appeared in the papers six months later. We will return to the subject of false advertising at the end of the chapter.

Here's one last example:

PROGRESSIVE SO. FLORIDA COMPANY seeks individual with experience in international trade. We are expanding overseas and need a person who can direct the company to the most profitable opportunities. Send salary requirements to Cheryl Spencer, Aerospace Systematics, Inc., 988 Sample Road, Coral Springs, FL 33305.

This rather modest ad by national standards drew 126 responses. These were pared down to eleven finalists, of whom five were actually invited for an interview.

What you can conclude from these examples is that "many are called, but few are chosen." Your reply to a help-wanted ad probably will be one of hundreds—and these hundreds must be reduced to some three to five finalists.

I'm going to show you how to "beat the system" so that you're one of the ones called in for an interview. The first step is to understand the process of hiring people through advertising.

How It Works

A Decision Maker decides that he or she needs to add someone to the staff. A job description is written. Approval is obtained to fill the slot. The budget for the position either already exists or is created. The opening is advertised on the company bulletin board to preserve at least the notion that the organization promotes from within. If no qualified person emerges, the Decision Maker thinks of all the outside people he or she knows, and if this does not produce a likely candidate, the DM then expands the search by telling friends and associates of the opening. If this step fails to produce results, the Decision Maker may then elect to retain an executive search firm, inform contingency searchers and/or employment agencies of the opening, or advertise for candidates.

If the decision is to advertise, the personnel manager discusses the job description with the DM to determine what qualifications the position calls for. This information forms the basis for the ad. The personnel manager or an assistant then writes the copy, which is the writer's impression of what the Decision Maker thinks the position requires. Sometimes the DM approves the wording of the copy, but not always. Either way, it makes little difference, because in the end there is usually only a slight relationship between the terms of the ad and the successful candidate.

To beat the system and become one of the 3 to 5 percent who are interviewed, you must understand what happens to your response when it arrives in the personnel department. It is sent to the Decision Maker, of course. Right? Wrong! If you were the president of the venture capital company in our second example, would you have the time to grapple with the write-ups of 900-odd hopefuls? Certainly not. The task of cutting down the responses to five or ten contenders is delegated by the DM to the personnel manager, who may, in turn, pass this responsibility on to the person who wrote the ad or even to the new clerk who was just hired and has yet to find the coffee machine. How does this person cull the candidates? What criteria are used?

THE WORDS IN THE AD.

The process of picking the five or ten responses that will be sent to the DM involves a simple matching of words . . . *those that have been submitted with those of the ad.* Therein you have the secret of getting interviews from advertisements. It is that simple. You can win an interview through any ad. The challenge is to be able to get the job offer once you are onstage. More on that later.

Needless to say, if you reply to an ad for a brain surgeon with all the right words when in reality you are a transmission repair specialist, your interview may prove to be embarrassing. Use some judgment, please, but do not err on the side of humility.

Ad Matching

To get the interview, you must match the words of your response to the words of the advertisement. Consider the following advertisement for a corporate staff accountant. The key words have been underlined.

**CORPORATE
STAFF ACCOUNTANT**

<u>Corporate Finance</u> department of an established, successful <u>multiplant electrical products manufacturer</u> needs a professional experienced in <u>general accounting</u>.

<u>Independent action</u> and <u>leadership</u> capabilities are required. Location is Indianapolis.

Requirements include 3 years in <u>general ledger</u>, <u>consolidations</u>, <u>payroll and related taxes</u>, <u>cash management</u>, and <u>cash forecasts</u>. Send resume in confidence.

Corporate Controller
Box P-48, *Indianapolis Times*

There are eleven key words and phrases in this ad:

1. corporate finance
2. multiplant
3. electrical products manufacturer
4. general accounting

5. independent action
6. leadership
7. general ledger
8. consolidations
9. payroll and related taxes
10. cash management
11. cash forecasts

On the following page is a response drafted by Jeremy Laslowe to match the wording of the ad. Note the underlined key phrases. As you can see, the words in this response are chosen to match the words of the advertisement. Granted, this approach is not very subtle, but subtlety is not the name of the game. You are after an interview. The delegated culler of the several hundred responses to this ad will be delighted to come across a candidate who so closely fits the requirements. Jeremy's reply will be on top of the five to ten letters that are submitted to the Decision Maker.

Let's review this letter in light of the resume rules that we discussed in Chapter 4. Laslowe's response is, in effect, a resume in letter form, chosen because it offers more flexibility for matching. But the same rules apply.

Resume Rule 1: Specialize Each Resume to Each Target
Obviously the reply is right on the mark.

Resume Rule 2: Keep the Resume to One Page
Check.

Resume Rule 3: Include a Company-Oriented Statement of Objective
The last statement in Laslowe's letter shows that he has the best interests of the company in mind.

Resume Rule 4: Include Accomplishments
Jeremy earned "a special bonus" and brought about "an increase in corporate earnings of 3 cents per share."

Resume Rule 5: Never State Salary Requirements
There is no mention of compensation either in the advertisement or in the response. If an ad asks for salary history, ignore it. If you carry out the word matching as described here, you will be interviewed whether you comply with the request for salary information or not.

Resume Rule 6: Indicate Your Age
The date Laslowe received his B.A. gives an approximate idea of his age.

Resume Rule 7: Put Pertinent Data Up Front
A B.A. from one of the finest business schools in the country is very important and is wisely used as Laslowe's lead-in.

Jeremy A. Laslowe
135 Fir Drive
Indianapolis, IN 46206
317-555-6742

October 16, 1990

Dear Sir or Madam,

I have a B.A. from the Wharton School (1973), and I am currently working toward an M.B.A.

My experience in <u>general accounting</u> spans seven years. I am presently on the <u>corporate staff</u> of Entoc Electronics, <u>manufacturers of electronic and electrical products</u> for commercial and industrial application. My career is presently roadblocked.

Entoc has <u>five operating divisions</u> at various locations. It has been my task to <u>consolidate</u> their individual reports into a corporate statement. In order to ensure compatible and meaningful results, it has been necessary to exercise <u>leadership</u> and to take <u>independent action</u> when representing the corporate office at these locations. The work included the merging of the financial practice of a recent acquisition with that of our company. The smoothness with which this was accomplished earned me a special bonus.

Prior to joining the corporate staff three years ago, I was Division Comptroller for our company's largest operating unit, the Switchmatic Division. There I managed all financial matters for the profit center, including <u>general ledger</u>, <u>payroll</u>, <u>payroll taxes</u>, <u>cash management</u>, and <u>cash forecasting</u>.

I recently implemented a uniform cash-flow analysis and cash-management system for the whole corporation that improved its return on investment, resulting in an increase in corporate earnings of 3 cents per share.

I believe my background and experience can help your company achieve its profit goals, and I request an interview.

Sincerely,

Jeremy A. Laslowe

Resume Rule 8: Avoid the Job-Hopper Image
Laslowe never lets the issue come up, since he describes his background in terms of functions and products.

Resume Rule 9: Omit Superfluous Information
Every word in this letter works toward the goal of being invited for an interview.

No Time for Humility

When Ed Hergenrather, the granddaddy of West Coast recruiters, encouraged me to make a career move, he described the new company as a leader in "transducers." I have never admitted this before, but I had to look up the word. I had no idea what the company's products were. It turned out that a transducer is "a device whereby energy is transmitted from one system to another system." The thrust of the new company was the design and manufacture of pressure gauges, temperature switches, accelerometers, gyroscopes, and similar devices. I had been working at the systems level at GE, where such devices had provided all the data that enabled the missiles to function, and so could relate my experience to the transducer, even though I didn't know the term. I got the job. Had I been overcome by humility and concluded that, since I did not understand transducers, I was obviously not qualified, I might have eliminated myself from the competition. As a vice president of the new company, I created opportunities in the marketplace that enabled it to grow from $25-million to $85-million in sales.

Lock your humility in a closet when responding to a job ad. If the company is after someone in your field, you will be able to do the word matching that earns you an interview. You do not have to be the world's greatest expert at every activity you mention when matching the words of the ad. You can cross that bridge when you meet the DM.

YOUR ONLY PURPOSE IN ANSWERING AN AD IS TO
GET AN INTERVIEW.

Go for it by using the matching technique. Remember this: 80 percent of the hiring decision is based on the person-to-person interview and not on the resume. Get the interview. In a later chapter, I'll tell you how to win the job offer once you are there.

Leapfrog the Competition

Remember Cheryl Spencer at the "Progressive So. Florida Company" whose ad I quoted earlier in the chapter? How about Mr. I. Gush from Chapter 4? It was in response to this ad that he sent his voluminous resume. Remember also that Gush did not get the job but I did. The scenario went like this.

I called Cheryl Spencer, told her I was very interested in the opportunity, and asked, "Who are your competitors?" She was very helpful. Then I called the competitors, told them I was a consultant to the aerospace industry (true), and asked them to describe their product lines and send me their literature. With this information I put together a flip-chart presentation for my interview, including references to competitors' catalogs and ads. I learned later that, despite the fact that there were two candidates ahead of me and two more to be interviewed after me, I had won the job on the spot. By doing a little homework, I leapfrogged the competition. That homework cost me about five phone calls and three or four hours of my time. I ended up president of the company. You, too, can leapfrog the competition if you make the effort.

The Singapore Connection

Here's an interesting ad:

GENERAL MANAGER
U.S. Multinational Pharmaceutical Company
Expanding to Singapore

Unique opportunity to manage a start-up joint venture and build to significant size and profitability by 1992. Work with partner, gain understanding of marketing priorities, distribution, and government procedures.

Candidate should have:

- Ability to converse in Mandarin and English
- Experience in Asia and interest in China
- Strong leadership and management skills
- Willingness to spend four years on assignment

Will consider non-Mandarin-speaking candidates having the other qualifications. Ample financial and professional rewards.

Box XYZ, the *Wall Street Journal*

This was a blind ad, and I challenged myself to identify and talk to the Decision Maker behind the box number. Within four days, I had him on the phone. In those four days, I had talked to six companies and three government agencies. I obtained key information from the Asian Desk at the State Department and from an executive secretary who knew it was not her company advertising and was willing to help in return for a line on the competition. (I later paid my dues by naming the company for her.) Actually, it was a rather easy piece of detective work. How many pharmaceutical companies would be starting a joint venture in Singapore at the same time?

While the other candidates were preparing their responses to the ad, I had already presented my case to the Decision Maker. I had bypassed the stack of resumes. You can do the same thing with blind ads that contain sufficient clues. The chapter on telephone techniques will help.

As it turned out, the position went to an internal candidate who was fluent in both English and Mandarin. I was never really sure I would have gone to Singapore for four years, but I would have liked to have to decide.

False Advertising

There is one other consideration when answering advertisements. All ads are not legitimate. Fly-by-night recruiters and employment agencies routinely run fake ads to gather resumes. Some companies are people-peddlers: they collect resumes and shop them around. If they get low on people worth peddling, they run an ad to build up their inventory. It generally reads something like this:

SALES MANAGER Rapidly growing Fortune 500 company has an outstanding opening for seasoned Sales Executive in stand-alone computers. Excellent benefits and location. Salary in the high $80s. Requires B.S. in engineering and willingness to travel.

Box 398, *Los Angeles Times*

The ad doesn't cost much and can easily be changed, depending on the fish to be netted. "Stand-alone computers" becomes "industrial controls," the B.S. a Ph.D. in nucleonics. Publishers have tried to stamp out this practice, but they really can't do much. The only way to identify these fakes is to monitor the classified section. Over a period of a few weeks, you may recognize the same format used for a variety of positions. That's the clue. Avoid these "opportunities" no matter how extraordinary they may sound unless you want your boss to know you are looking—because, through these people, your resume could very well end up on your boss's desk.

59

You now have everything you need to travel the advertisement pathway. Applying what you've learned in this chapter, you'll be able to answer any ad you choose and get a job interview. In the next chapter, you will find out about the remaining pathways: recruiters, employment agencies, and the job application.

Chapter 6

Recruiters, Agencies, and Applications

"Paying someone to find a job for you is like hiring someone to say your prayers."

This chapter deals with the remaining pathways to your new job. They are executive search firms, employment agencies, and the employment application itself. The discussion will also touch upon career counselors, outplacement, and Forty-Plus. It is important to understand the nature of these pathways so you can travel them to your advantage.

Executive Search Firms

Executive search firms, also known as headhunters, can be important in your campaign for better employment, but never depend on them entirely. The *Directory of Executive Recruiters* (Kennedy Publications, Fitzwilliam, N.H.) lists firms working in this field.

Search firms come in two basic types: retained and contingency. Companies hire retained firms on an exclusive basis to fill key openings. They pay a fee based on the compensation level of the position to be filled, usually 30 to 35 percent of its annual salary. Other payment schemes include flat-rate and time-and-expenses. The company usually pays a retainer of one third to start the search, another third after an agreed-upon milestone is passed, and the remainder when the successful candidate reports for work. However, some firms are paid the full fee just for trying hard, even if no one is hired. Most retained firms are also reimbursed for their out-of-pocket expenses, such as travel, lodging, telephone calls, and postage.

Contingency searchers work on a bounty basis. They are paid if and when one of the candidates they have presented is hired. Fees are equivalent to a percentage of the hiring salary, ranging from a low of 15 percent to a high of 35 percent. There are about 1,500 such firms listed in the *Directory of Executive Recruiters,* but there are many name changes from year to year. The contingency search business, like real estate, is always in a very fluid state.

Retained Search

Once the retained search firm receives an exclusive contract to recruit candidates for a key position, the search is assigned to a senior associate who will be responsible for finding a person the client will hire. First, the associate will go to the search firm's files to see if any suitable candidates are already there. The files are organized in two ways: by function (finance, engineering, manufacturing, etc.) and by industry (petroleum, retail goods, automotive, aerospace, etc.). If no likely candidates are on the files, the recruiter will explore the client's competition, as mentioned in Chapter 2, and do a number of other things not important to us here, until the position is filled.

When a resume arrives at a recruiter's office, the file clerk makes two copies and opens a folder for one of them. This folder is circulated to everyone in the office. The original and the other copy go into the files, one under function and the other under industry, as described above. It should be very clear to the clerk which function and specialty you have targeted, so that the copies of your resume are filed where they can do you the most good. If it is not clear that your field is exterminating, your resume may reside for decades in undertaking. This is yet another reason why you should be specific about pinpointing functions and specialties on your resume.

The covering letter is stapled to the inside front of the folder, where it will not be in the way. Nobody reads it. Even so, 999 resumes out of 1,000 are accompanied by covering letters. They all start with the reason for writing. There are as many reasons offered for sending a resume as there are excuses for speeding made to the highway patrol.

- Your search firm was recommended to me by . . .
- In the course of your search assignments, you may have a need for . . .
- I am writing to you because of my experience in . . .
- Could I help one of your clients in . . . ?
- I understand your firm deals with clients seeking . . .
- Due to a recent reorganization, . . .

Here are two from members of the egotists' group:

- I think you will agree that it is unusual to find a highly competent technical person who also has strength in . . .
- It has been about four months since I sent you my executive profile . . . (In other words, "Get off your duff and do something for me!")

Who knows what the rest of these letters said? A recruiter will move on, spending 3 seconds on the resume to see if it is of any interest. But if you absolutely must send a covering letter, pattern it on this one:

Dear Search Consultant:

Please consider the enclosed resume in connection with any present or future search assignments in General Management of Retail Soft Goods.

My current base salary is $125,000, and last year's bonus was $50,000. I will relocate for the right opportunity.

If you think that I might meet the needs of one of your clients, please call me at 414-555-9677.

Thank you for your consideration.

When a folder is circulated and the person described is recognized as a possible fit with an ongoing search, the recruiter responsible will make another copy of the resume, claim the recruit as his or her own, and be on the phone with the person immediately. If the person does not match a current assignment but might meet an anticipated requirement, some senior associates will keep a copy of the resume for their own files. If neither of these things happens, the only action will be the filing of the resume by function and industry. Your covering letter will go unanswered, as will follow-up phone calls. (Recruiters *do* answer letters and phone calls from clients for the simple reason that it is the clients who pay them.) Don't be affronted by what seems to be rejection. It is not personal. Everyone is treated the same.

Retained recruiters want to build a reputation for finding good people fast. This is what they are paid for. They have no interest in helping people find jobs unless these people happen to fit an assigned search. Their time and energy is spent ferreting out viable candidates. Any distracting activities are eliminated.

My search firm used to be listed in the yellow pages and as a result received many unsolicited resumes each month, complete with covering letters. Most announced plans to move to Florida and requested help in finding employment in the state. The writers had

63

no way of knowing that I had no clients in Florida and could not help. Many followed up with a phone call, wondering why I hadn't called or answered their letter. Even after I explained that I couldn't help and why, some kept pressing and even became obstreperous. At this point I asked if the check was in the mail, since they obviously thought I was working for them.

One More Resume Rule

For your resume to have the maximum effect with a recruiter, it must contain your age and salary requirements. There is no way a recruiter will present your background to a client without these two pieces of information at the ready. Granted, if your resume meets all the search requirements but is missing age and salary, the searcher will still call you. However, if you almost fit but nothing is known of your age and compensation level, you might not get that call. You could miss an opportunity to sell yourself to someone who could help you on your way to a Decision Maker.

You may have thought that the Resume Rule to End All Resume Rules was the end of resume rules, but I lied:

Resume Rule 10:
The Resume You Send to Recruiters Must Contain Your Age and Salary Requirements

By all means, execute a complete campaign by sending your resume to retained recruiters. The resume cannot be aimed as precisely as your rifle-shot letters or your answers to advertisements, but you can focus on the target to a degree. The *Directory of Executive Recruiters* identifies search firms by their industry specialties, such as construction, oil and gas extraction, paper and allied products, etc., allowing you to develop resumes that emphasize your background and experience in ways that match specific firms' specialties. Placing your credentials with a retained recruiter is relatively confidential, because you will not be shopped around your industry. However, there are some pitfalls to be avoided.

Be Inquisitive

When on a retained search, the recruiter must keep the client satisfied that progress is being made. When fully qualified candidates are difficult to find, marginal people are sometimes presented as window dressing, either to give evidence that the recruiter is working or to make candidates who have been presented already look better by comparison. I was once the "pigeon" in such a deception. The client was in the San Fernando Valley, a $25 taxi ride from the headhunter's office in Los Angeles. I was on a trip from the East and agreed to the meeting. It took place in a bar, on bar stools, and it lasted about 30 minutes. After the first 5 minutes, it was obvious that there was no fit, and on the ride back I began to realize what had taken place. The recruiter was having trouble finding the right candidate and needed to demonstrate effort. I was chosen as window dressing.

My advice is to be very inquisitive when a recruiter wants to set up an interview for you. Ask:

- Is this a retained search?
- How long have you had this assignment?
- What is the target salary?
- What else goes with the compensation package?
- Who is the Decision Maker?
- Will the interview be with him or her?
- Is the position vacant, and, if so, why?
- Is there an incumbent, and, if so, why is this person leaving?
- How many candidates have you presented to date?
- Why were they not chosen?
- Are any of them still under consideration?

The answers you get will equip you to judge whether the interview will be worth it or not. If the recruiter will not or cannot answer these questions to your satisfaction, let the opportunity pass to someone else. Just asking will ensure that you are not presented as window dressing. The searcher will pick a less well informed pigeon.

If it is not a retained search, your recruiter is not in charge, and there are probably many other candidates being presented through other headhunters. The position even could have been filled without your searcher's knowledge. If the search has been open for several months, you could be up against a very fickle client. The compensation information will enable you to decide very quickly if you want to participate or not. The title of the Decision Maker will tell you the level and importance of the slot in the company. If the interview is not with the DM, forget it. If you're not being considered seriously enough to meet with the DM, you will be wasting your time with the personnel department.

Information on why the vacancy has occurred is helpful. If the incumbent has quit, you may want to find that person for an informative debriefing as you become more interested in the job. The number of candidates presented suggests how difficult the search has been and also how particular the client is. Both factors tend to raise your price if you become the successful candidate.

If the search has been open for some time and a multitude of candidates has been paraded by the DM, it may be that the company is just shopping. If the headhunter will level with you about the ways in which previous candidates broke their picks, you will be usefully forewarned. If one or more candidates are still under consideration, you know your chances are reduced, but that can be offset by your learning why they have not been chosen and making up their deficiencies when you are interviewed.

Accept an invitation to meet with the DM by saying, "OK, I am willing to invest my time if your client is willing to cover my travel and living expenses." With retained searchers, this point is usually obvious, but why not be sure right from the start?

Retained searchers can help. They do place people. Include them in your program; just don't put all your chips on their number.

Contingency Search

Contingency search firms have the same objective as those doing retained work: to earn fees by finding candidates for companies willing to pay for the service. They handle resumes in the same way, except that individual recruiters are more inclined to build up their inventories of job candidates by copying the resumes that are circulated. The major difference between the two types of firms is the system of payment: contingency firms get paid only when a candidate reports for work. There are other differences. Contingency firms are, in effect, bounty hunters, and they will peddle people. In addition to submitting candidates to companies with known openings, they will present people with impressive credentials in hopes of creating a need. Their business is something of a numbers game, based on the principle that if you throw enough mud up against a wall, some of it will stick. The industry rule of thumb is that ten interviews result in one placement.

Another important difference is that contingency searches are not carried out on an exclusive basis, which means there can be several recruiters working to fill the same position. You can never know the real status of the search, whether it's how many candidates are in the picture or even whether the job has been filled recently.

There is also the consideration of confidentiality. Your resume in the files of a retained searcher is relatively secure. It will only be exposed when there is the possibility of your fitting an exclusive search. However, your resume in the hands of a contingency company can and most likely will be circulated all over your industry.

At a recent trade show I was approached by a candidate who

announced, in strictest confidence, that she was ready to make a move. She swore me to absolute secrecy. She would authorize me to submit her name when I had given her the details of a possible fit, but not before. Despite all her precautions, when I got back to my office I found that one of my sources had sent *me* a copy of her resume. She was aghast, but discussion revealed that she had given a copy of the resume to a contingency searcher, and it obviously had been peddled. Who knew how many other copies were out there?

The rule in the contingency business is that the company that first submits the successful candidate is the one that gets paid. One copy of a resume is sent by Over-the-Rainbow Recruiting and reaches Epitome Fabrics, Inc., on Wednesday. Another copy of the same resume arrives from Sunshine Searchers the next day. The candidate is hired, and Over-the-Rainbow gets the bounty. If ten interviews are necessary for one placement, and the first one to submit the successful candidate earns the fee, you can understand that the name of the game in contingency work is to throw as much mud as fast as possible; that is, submit as many candidates as possible before the competition finds them. If you are "on the beach" with a high urgency factor, all this should matter very little. Crank out the resumes to the contingency firms (without covering letter) and take whatever results they can produce. All it will cost you is time and stamps. On the other hand, if you cannot risk your resume ending up on your boss's desk, be more cautious.

When invited to interview, ask the same questions you would pose to a retained recruiter. Be aware that the contingency folks will try to get you to interview first with the personnel department far more often than will their retained counterparts. Whether you agree to this or not will depend, once again, on your urgency factor.

The contingency people are no better or worse than the retained firms when it comes to returning phone calls or answering letters. Their criterion is the same. If responding will help them make money, they will respond. In defense of both types of recruiters, it must be said that getting clients to act is sometimes very difficult. It always takes much more time than expected to set interview dates, receive feedback, and get decisions, and the recruiter should not be blamed for these delays.

Take Your Recruiter's Lead

On the assumption that you are working with a qualified recruiter, follow his or her instructions. Your interests very nearly coincide. The recruiter wants to get the position filled in order to get paid; you want the job offer and will accept it if it is satisfactory. The good recruiter knows more than you do about the process of getting an offer and is familiar with details about the client company, including the preferences and idiosyncrasies of the Decision Maker. Your headhunter can also provide helpful input from previous candidates' interviews. Also, if you are in the hands of a good recruiter, you will receive coaching on how to handle the interview.

One very important step is to call your recruiter immediately after an interview so he or she will have your input before talking to the DM. This lets your coach know if there were any rough spots that can be smoothed when following up with the client.

Employment Agencies

There are thousands upon thousands of employment agencies, and hundreds come and go every day. Some have as many as thirty employment counselors, and some are one-person businesses. They will give you a sales pitch about how your qualifications will be analyzed so they can place you in the slot that is just right, when, in fact, what they do is send your resume out and hope someone, anyone, will hire you. None of them do anything that you cannot do better on your own. Paying someone to find a job for you is like hiring someone to say your prayers.

Employment agencies operate on the same principle as do the contingency search firms: the more resumes they send out, the more candidates they can expect to place and the more money they will earn. Fees are sometimes paid by the companies, but, as never happens with search firms, fees must sometimes be paid by the unwary candidates themselves. The fee is based on the position and can be as high as 60 percent of the first month's pay. On this basis, if you capture a job that pays $20,000 a year through an agency, it could cost you $1,000. You can buy a lot of word processing, many long-distance phone calls, and loads of first-class stamps with $1,000.

Another significant difference between employment agencies and contingency search firms is the level and location of the jobs they handle. Generally speaking, as of this writing search firms are concerned with positions nationwide that pay over $45,000 a year. Employment agencies will tell you that they operate nationwide and handle positions up to and over the $100,000 level. In reality, they operate locally with jobs that pay under $40,000 (mostly well under).

Perhaps an employment agency can help you, but make sure you are considered for fee-paid positions only. This is the term used to indicate that the hiring company will pay the agency's fee. Do not sign any agreement with an employment agency.

DO NOT SIGN ANY AGREEMENT WITH AN
EMPLOYMENT AGENCY.

That way you do not have to be wary of the fine print. If you are placeable in a fee-paid job, it will not make any difference whether you sign an agreement or not; the agency will still present you.

These firms come in all forms, and it is difficult to separate the professionals from the phoneys, who are sued and sue for all sorts of malfeasance. In a job search, you don't have time for litigation. Why take the chance? Don't sign that agreement! Letting an agency place you in a fee-paid job is OK; otherwise, do it yourself. It will be done better, in less time, and at a fraction of the cost, and most likely you will end up with a better job.

Flimflam for a Fee

We have now arrived at the biggest rip-off in the employment business. Its practitioners, who should be distinguished from the many legitimate career counselors on college campuses and elsewhere, go by many names: career counselors, executive career counselors, career consultants, executive career consultants, career guidance counselors, executive career guidance counselors, and on and on. Their scam is to convince you that, without a doubt, their treatment will get you a new and better job at a much higher salary without delay. The rip-off is that you pay them up front and usually end up with nothing much more than a draft of your resume.

The process usually begins with a presentation given by a "senior executive" with a high-sounding title like Vice President of Counseling. In reality, this person is in the job because of an ability to close a sale. Think of the door-to-door salesman trying to sell you an encyclopedia or solar heating and you have the picture. The "closer" has a sincere manner and projects the image of a very mature and distinguished person. He or she outlines a program that will have you in your new, high-paying position in a matter of days, or weeks at the most. You are told that career counseling will be designed to fit your special qualifications and requirements, that you will get all kinds of help, and that the program is guaranteed to work because of the quality of the training and the network of employer contacts the company has developed.

The steps of the counseling process are outlined as follows:

- An in-depth analysis of your career.
- Identification of the strengths, skills, and abilities that are to be marketed, along with notation of any weaknesses and ways of covering them.
- Development of career objectives.
- Assistance in the preparation of a resume.
- Instruction in networking.
- Arrangement of appointments.
- Coaching in the techniques of interviewing and salary negotiation.
- Continued counseling for a period of twelve months.

At this point the senior executive must make a very important decision. She or he must make a judgment as to how much the traffic will bear and price your program accordingly. One of them priced me at $1,200 and judged an associate of mine to be worth $3,000, no doubt because he was sporting a very good imitation of a Rolex watch. You will be given a price somewhere between $1,000 and $5,000 (yes, $5,000!), depending on the estimate of your ability to pay. You will be offered "easy" terms of one half to begin with and the balance in thirty days. A credit card imprinter will be at the ready. Terms will not be extended beyond a month, because after thirty days or so you will realize you have been had and won't want to pay. The con job will have become obvious. You will have a draft of a resume based on what you already know (which is only what you have told them), you will have been reminded constantly that you are very employable, you will have received much backslapping encouragement, and you won't be as near to a new job as if you had done it yourself.

If you are lucky, the "closer" will also be your counselor. If not, and you are turned over to another senior executive for counseling, you will have become the equivalent of a hockey puck. You will, of course, expect the counselor to make good on all the "closer's" promises; however, you may find that these promises were never made clear to your counselor, and all you will get is what the fine print of the contract stipulates. You can be slapped back and forth from counselor to "closer," but you will not score. It's the counselors who scored when you wrote out the check.

Should you ask how the program is guaranteed, the senior executive, with much arm waving, will explain that the guarantee resides in the fact that the program always works. When asked if you can have the guarantee in writing and whether your money will be refunded if no job materializes, the answer again is accompanied by much arm waving. You will be told that a refund would be made, except that your cooperation is not guaranteed, and thus the counselor has no control over the ultimate success of the search.

I have evaluated four of these outfits in person by submitting to their sales pitches, and I have also debriefed four associates who were unfortunate enough to have written checks. One of these associates was presented with a $5,000 tab, and the company went under before his resume was drafted. When last I heard from him, he was still trying to get his money back.

The programs I evaluated were all about the same, but there were some interesting gimmicks. Some had framed awards all over the walls. Some programs were supported by textbooks, one of which suggested that a great thing to do is check the papers to see what conventions are in town and circulate in the lobbies of host hotels to make valuable contacts. If you are unemployed and have to depend on that level of strategy, be sure you have funds to carry you through a long search.

One local firm guaranteed in writing that they would arrange ten "appointments." This term was designed to be interpreted as "interviews," when in reality it meant meetings with local shills who had no interest in hiring. Another firm came complete with a bearded Ph.D. in psychology who would "analyze your career in depth" to point you at exactly the right job.

The most masterful con job I encountered was carried out by a firm that had offices nationwide. The office I visited was staffed by an attractive secretary and an executive in a Brooks Brothers suit. I had expected conference and study rooms and counselors poised to help me at the drop of a check, but these two were it. The "closer" explained the program, which was basically like all the rest: career analysis, resume writing, training in networking and interviewing, etc. One major difference was that a staff of placement experts would be working on my behalf by actively presenting me to potential employers. The second difference was that all counseling and placement work would be done at their corporate headquarters in New York City. I would be flown there at their expense.

- The charge was $4,000.
- I should write a check at once.
- I should pay for the airline ticket.
- If I was accepted into the program, the airline fare would be refunded (from my $4,000, of course).
- If I was not accepted, the $4,000 would be refunded.

Obviously, no one was ever refused.

This outfit was, in reality, a contingency recruiter with a gimmick that conned unsuspecting job hunters into paying exorbitant fees for the privilege of having their resumes included in the company's files. As with other contingency searchers, a fee would be collected when someone hired one of their people, so the company would make out twice on a candidate. However, as with any search firm, a resume could reside in the files for years without any action, and that is most likely all I would have gotten for my four grand. Happily this scam was exposed at the national level, and the company was forced out of business.

My first appraisal of career counseling schemes was that they were aimed at the middle-income market, trying to convince people making $15,000–$20,000 that counseling services would win them at least $10,000 more. Since then, however, I have noticed some very interesting ads in the national newspapers. They go something like this:

> "Announcement is made of the first Marketing Services and Career Enhancement Program exclusively for proven executive-level personnel. Three years in development, this program is for $90,000–$300,000 aspirants who . . ."

The words go on to suggest that many high-level placements are made. Maybe there is some good in these programs for people at that level who have been fired without the benefit of outplacement and have an ego that doesn't permit them to sign up with the Forty-Plus program we will be looking at. I'm sure that the fee for these people would be $20,000 and up, but that may not seem exorbitant in their pay brackets, even if all they really get is someone to talk to.

If you decide to satisfy your curiosity and submit yourself to the career counseling con job, here is your reply when the pitchman asks you to agree to a contract—it should be entirely Pavlovian, triggered by the words "sign here"—"You assure me that the program works, and I assure you that I want a new job. Why don't we trust each other, and I will pay you when I get hired?" This sounds like a reasonable proposal, but it will cause senior executive and credit card imprinter to vanish like smoke.

Outplacement

Outplacement is a polite term for a service that may be made available to you when you are fired. It is really a sop to the conscience of the company that has let you go: "We certainly treated old Charlie right when we fired him. We gave him a gold watch and outplacement." It costs your former company the equivalent of from 12 to 15 percent of your annual salary. There are many reputable firms conducting outplacement, so if it is offered to you, go for it.

You will be provided with a counselor, telephones, and word processing services: all of the tools you need. The counselor may be a young person just out of college or a retired executive, depending on the firm and your turn of the cards. There are some excellent outplacement firms, and then there are others whose counselors have little job-finding experience but are armed to some extent with theory. It makes no difference, because the important things for you are the telephone and word processor that will enable you to keep the pathways busy. You will have the use of a phone number that is manned during business hours and is answered, "Executive Offices." You will have people keeping the computer busy with specialized versions of your resume, running mail campaigns for you, providing copying services, etc. Outplacement means that a multifaceted office is at your disposal. Use it. When you don't score first off, keep using the office. Don't become discouraged. Keep the telephone, word processor, and secretaries busy on the pathways of your program. If you are unfortunate enough to need outplacement but fortunate enough to have it, use it and keep using it!

Forty-Plus

If you are unemployed, 40 years old or older, and without outplacement, enroll immediately in the nearest branch of Forty-Plus. This is a self-help and help-each-other program for those looking for work, and it even has a placement service. There are chapters in all major cities, and you can find them in the white pages. The services are like those of outplacement, except that members are counseled by fellow members. They take turns manning the phones, do their own word processing, and so on. The fees are minimal, just enough to cover overheads. Each participant donates one day a week to help run the office.

I graduated in 1980 from the Los Angeles chapter of Forty-Plus, where my duty assignment was the counseling committee. The program was a great experience. It was there I received my first exposure to word processing on a pioneering NBI system. The support from other members was extraordinary, and many are now close friends.

Back in those days, the basic approach at Forty-Plus was a Carl Boll broadcast letter. I imagine it has changed since then to a rifle-shot tactic, but this need not concern you. Join Forty-Plus and simply implement what you've learned here. You will have all the facilities you need, plus support from all sides.

Similar programs are being developed elsewhere, among them the Professional Employment Network sponsored by the State of California, and a program that is currently being piloted in fifteen cities by the American Association of Retired Persons. Any program of this sort is very valuable as an operating base from which to journey down the pathways. But don't confuse the programs described here with the employment services of the various states. Not to run these other programs down, but the need to handle a vast number of candidates working at all levels of the economy makes it impossible for these services to provide the same atmosphere of self-help and help for each other.

Employment Applications

Employment applications should be treated as very important, because, quite simply, they are. Most are not completed with the care they deserve. This is due partly to the circumstances under which applications are often completed: in the company lobby with a six-month-old copy of *Time* on your knee for a desk and a borrowed ballpoint pen to write with.

There are two rules to remember about filling out applications:

- Make them neat.
- Make them factual.

Consider the application to be a special form of resume and apply the ten resume rules as much as the form will allow. Be particularly sensitive to Resume Rule 9, in which you were cautioned to avoid the job-hopper image. It is very easy to come across as a job hopper, since the application can ask for all your jobs since birth in reverse chronological order. If this is a problem, use artistic license, and, as much as possible, present your background in broad function and specialty terms, as in the revised Frank Torez resume. Do, however, describe your last two or three positions, because they are the ones of real interest and the ones that will be checked, if any are.

Ideally, you should drop by the company a few days before an interview to get a copy of the employment application so that you won't have to complete it in the lobby. Take it and the personnel manager's name home with you. Make a couple of copies that you can use for penciled rough drafts. Complete the form with the resume rules in the front of your mind. Revise and re-revise. When satisfied, do the neat final draft. If your handwriting and printing are as bad as mine, get a friend to go final for you. Then sign the form and mail it to the personnel manager, or bring it with you when you come in for the interview.

When you get a job, the application will be in your personnel file forever. This is no place to include erroneous dates or imaginary credentials. No falsehoods, please. Present the simple truth in a favorable light.

My application education came when I was being considered for a position as a vice president. Frankly, I felt I was highly qualified. The interview had gone well, and I expected an offer. Toward the end of the interview, I was asked to fill out a lengthy application. By the time I was through erasing and scratching out, the form was a mess. It did not seem to be that important, so instead of asking for another application that could be filled in neatly, I submitted the sloppy copy. I did not get the offer and learned later that the president of the company placed a great deal of weight on the employment application, which he had designed personally.

The importance of this pathway will vary with your circumstances. It is perhaps most important at entry level, although in the case of that vice president job it turned out to be crucial.

Where to Put the Emphasis

You are now familiar with the six pathways to your new job: friends, associates, letters, ads, recruiters, and employment applications. Each one is important. Where should you place the emphasis to achieve maximum effectiveness? The answer lies in your particular situation, but there are some generalizations that can help you decide. At this point, I must digress for a while from the real world into theory, because there are no statistical data to substantiate the observations and conclusions that follow, only my thirty years of experience.

Employment applications have great relative importance in the early years of your career. This is because you have not yet established a track record, and the written data constitute the main basis for hiring. Sometimes candidates are put on the payroll on the strength of their application without ever having had an in-person interview. Recruiting on college campuses is sometimes done on this basis; this was the case with my first job after college. Someone from personnel supervises the completion of an employment application, and the person is hired without ever meeting the Decision Maker who will be his or her boss. Skilled workers can be put on the payroll in the same way, especially during the start-up of a new project. So if you are in the age group where this matters most, pay proper attention to the employment application and remember the rules: neat, factual, and in keeping with the resume rules.

As age increases, so does the importance of the friends pathway, until, at the senior-citizen level, it becomes almost the only path available. A friend can give you a job or provide such a strong recommendation that you score. Associates can do the same, but not to the same extent.

Your salary level will have some effect on which pathway you emphasize. Generally speaking, recruiters, particularly retained searchers, will be more important to those with annual salaries of over $50,000. And remember that the importance of the employment application, after peaking in the early years, does not decrease in importance with either age or salary level.

Chapter 7

Selecting the Successful Candidate

"On a job search, allow peeks under the blanket on your good side only."

There are two distinct aspects to the selection of the successful candidate. The "Miss America process" applies from the time of your first overture to the moment when you win the job offer. When you get to the interview stage, you also become subject to the workings of what I call the "Decision Maker's code."

The Miss America Process

The "Miss America process" refers to the successive weeding out of hopefuls according to their relative defects. The one who's left is declared the winner. Imagine that you have a bushel basket of tomatoes and have been assigned the task of picking the best one. You will sort them by setting aside first those that have the most obvious flaws, then those with more subtle flaws, until you have narrowed the candidates down to the four or five least imperfect. Then you will look at these few more closely and choose "the best one." The least flawed may or may not be the best one for cooking or canning, but that is a weakness in the system that must be accepted. A bruised tomato of the correct ripeness would be better for a salad than an immature one without a blemish. But if you are the bruised tomato with salad ambitions, you will have to conceal the flaw and emphasize your good flavor. The message is simply to conceal your bruises.

The thought of knowingly concealing flaws may cause you mental anguish. Be reminded that your objective is to get an offer for the position of your choice, not to confess your sins. You want to provide a peek under the blanket just sufficient to convince the Decision Maker to choose you. Nothing more. The pathway to a better job is no place to play "show and tell." If this concept causes you even the slightest moral discomfort, be reminded that for years after you are in your new job, you and your boss will be playing mutual "show and tell," and he or she will certainly have as much to reveal or conceal as you do. I have worked for a boss who turned out to have a serious drinking problem and another who hired me while under a grand jury investigation that finally put him in the slammer and the company out of business. Somehow these flaws did not surface during the interviewing and hiring process. It seems only fair that the candidate should be able to enjoy the same sanctuary.

About Flaws

In the candidate selection process, a flaw is anything negative. In Chapter 4 you were cautioned to keep your resume to one page and avoid any unnecessary information.

- Resume Rule 2: Keep the Resume to One Page.
- Resume Rule to End All Resume Rules: Omit Superfluous Information.

The principle is a simple one: relate only details that specifically enhance your chances of getting an invitation to interview, at the same time reducing the risk of introducing negatives or flaws. This means omitting obvious things like your participation in dangerous sports or controversial organizations; you can skip the glossy photograph, too. However, extraneous information of a less obviously negative sort also can sow doubts in the mind of the recipient that you cannot anticipate. Why take the chance? The Miss America process works by identifying reasons to eliminate rather than reasons to retain. This may sound cynical, but it is the way of the world. Minimize your chances of being culled along the way to the job offer by providing only information pertinent to that objective.

> *You've got to Ac-cent-tchu-ate The Positive,*
> *E-lim-my-nate the negative,*
> *Latch on to the affirmative,*
> *Don't mess with Mister Inbetween.*

These song lyrics by Johnny Mercer summarize the approach you should take throughout your job campaign. Let this attitude permeate everything: resumes, letters, phone conversations, and interviews. Most of the time, before meeting the DM in person, you will be contacted by phone. Phone conversations are really phone interviews, providing the cullers with chances to eliminate you, and you with openings to change difficult questions into opportunities. Specific training on how to take charge of the telephone interview will be given in Chapter 11. Right now, the concentration is on being positive.

Following is a list of what I call "opportunity questions," along with sample responses to stimulate your own thinking. Others describe these as "critical" or "stress" questions because the answers can reveal negatives. I look at them as opportunities to make a positive statement and thereby distinguish yourself from the competition. But in order to turn them into opportunities, you must rehearse your answers to these questions before anyone has a chance to ask them. Don't risk ad-libbing in front of the Decision Maker. If you can think of other questions that are particularly pertinent to your own situation, add them to the list and practice your answers.

OPPORTUNITY QUESTIONS

1. What did you like most about your last job? What did you like least?

"I liked the challenges and the chance to beat the competition. I really liked everything. I was concerned that cost controls were not strict enough." (Something very positive and then a very positive negative. All management is in favor of apple pie, motherhood, and cost control.)

2. In your last job, what were your accomplishments? Your failures?

"My record as a loan officer was the best in the branch. I had the lowest percentage of defaults even though I managed one of the largest portfolios. I may have been a little too conservative." (The latter is another positive negative. Bankers get their jollies from being conservative.)

3. What are your thoughts about your last employer?

"It is a great company, and they treated me very well. I liked it very much." (Never, never, never say anything NEGATIVE here.)

4. What were your boss's strengths? Weaknesses?

"She had an outstanding ability to get to the heart of the problem and to rally the organization to solve it. She set very high personal standards, and I always felt she was too hard on herself." (The positive negative again.)

5. What did your subordinates think of you?

"They will tell you I was the best supervisor they ever had."

This is a good place to pause and talk about your moral upbringing again. The greatest liability in an effective job campaign is humility. One of the definitions of "humble" is "having or showing a consciousness of one's defects." Being conscious of your defects and showing them is hardly the correct approach to the DM—quite the opposite. You must be well aware of your abilities and display them openly and with conviction. Remember, "It ain't bragging if it's true."

Sometimes that puritan ethic may urge you to demonstrate that, after all, you are only human and to admit to a couple of faults. Never, never, never give in to that urge! Do not reveal that you were ever fired, flunked, demoted, or debunked; drunk, disorderly, or thrown out bodily; passed over, under, or guilty of blunder. On a job search, allow peeks under the blanket on your good side only. Save the rest for "show and tell" *after you are on the payroll,* and then let your new boss go first and stay ahead of you.

6. What qualities do you look for in hiring staff?

"I look for people who are committed to excellence in their job, people who have demonstrated in the past their desire to be the very best." (This is more orthodoxy that no DM can fault. If you get more specific, you risk stepping on invisible toes. Never give such responses as "I like graduates of Princeton," "Give me a good Baptist every time," or "I find ex-Marines make the best supervisors." Your DM may be ex–Air Force, a Yalie, or a Presbyterian.)

7. How do you feel about firing people?

"Firing people has always been a last resort with me. I am convinced I can put anyone in the right job if I try hard enough. However, firing is sometimes necessary on ethical grounds."

8. How would you evaluate your present or most recent company?

"I feel it treats its employees very well." (This is really a repeat of question 3, and you may be asked similar questions several times, for the DM wants a reading on what you might say after leaving his or her company. Even if you were fired because you believed the internal theft you uncovered should be reported to the District Attorney, always respond with a positive remark.)

9. Have you helped reduce costs? How?

"Yes. I revised our financial reports, eliminating three and reducing our computer time by 15 percent."

10. If you have been self-employed, why are you giving it up? Did the business fail?

"The business did not fail. It has reached a point at which investment capital is needed, and I'm selling it rather than go through that hassle."

11. Describe an occasion on which your work was criticized. On which it was praised.

"During the hectic days of completing the industrial complex contract, our customer became concerned that the schedule would not be met. As project manager, I was called on the carpet by the company president. At the time, I was not able to convince him or our customer that I had provided an adequate contingency plan to ensure that the schedule would be met. In the end, we met the schedule and, I might add, came in under budget, which made everyone very happy." (This is a sort of reverse positive negative.)

12. Why aren't you earning more at your age?

"I haven't thought much about that. I guess it's because of the time I spent in the Peace Corps. I made a three-year commitment after my training."

13. What do you look for in a job?

"I look for a chance to help the company in a job where I can get enjoyment from doing what I am good at." (This one will appeal to any DM at any level.)

14. What are your long-range objectives? Your short-range objectives?

"In the long run, I would like to move into your job when you move up. In the short run, I aim to be the best administrative assistant in your company." (This one can be tricky. You have to look ambitious but not overly so. You must be careful that the DM does not see you as a potential threat to his or her job. A general answer of the sort given in the example makes it clear that you want to see the DM promoted, and you want to do a good job for him or her. These number among those "good things," like apple pie and motherhood, that no one can interpret as being negative. The approach may seem audacious, but your objective is to get the job offer, not to be subtle.)

15. What is your philosophy of management?

"I believe the responsibility of management is to be so skillful that each staff member is in exactly the right position to get the job done." (Resist the urge to get on the soapbox. You never know where the DM's sensitivities lie. Keep it simple. Avoid statements like "Frankly, I think modern management theory stinks. I believe in laying out the work to be done and hiring the people to do it . . . and if they don't do it, I'll get others who will!")

16. What are your strengths? Your weaknesses?

"I believe my greatest strength is consistently meeting my commitments. I sometimes err on the side of being overly optimistic, planning too much work for a given period of time. Then I find myself having to put out extra effort, but my commitments are always met." (This question is very popular. All it needs is the standard treatment.)

17. How old are you?

"I'm 50 years old." (This is an illegal question. If it's asked, you can sue the DM for breaking the law, lie, or simply state your age. If you sue, you can forget working for that company and perhaps any other company in the area. If you lie and are hired, it will forever limit your career with that company when the truth comes out. And it always does. So the only way is to state your age and go on to win the job.)

18. What would you do differently in your career if given the chance?

"I wish I had taken the Dale Carnegie training earlier than I did, because it proved so valuable in the work I was doing for the company." (More apple pie and motherhood.)

19. How would you rate yourself as a professional? As an executive?

"I consider myself to be one of the top people in my profession. I have to turn new clients away because of my work load. This is because of my reputation for being thorough and accurate in my accounting, auditing, and tax service and particularly because of my ability to handle the IRS. One of the things I do best as an executive is motivating my staff to make that extra effort." (Be sure you do not let any humility sneak into this one.)

20. Are you able to work under pressure, deadlines, and so on?

"Yes." (A simple "yes" or "no" is the best answer to some questions. We will return to this point later.)

21. What business, character, and credit references can you give us?

"Until we are both certain that this is the right position for me, I think you will understand that I do not want to bother the people who have agreed to act as my references." (You will get special instruction on how to answer this question in Chapter 15.)

22. Are you in good health?

"Yes." (Many companies require a pre-employment physical examination. They will get the details then. No need to scare them off now. They may get to like you in spite of your African jungle rot.)

23. How would you describe your personality?

"I believe that I am quietly confident and that I relate well to management and to my peers." (Say nice things. Don't go humble here either.)

24. Are you willing to take a lie detector test?

"Yes, on three conditions: that I approve the tester, that I am permitted to record the session, and that you take the same test and we share our results." (Lie detector tests are now out of fashion, but I used to enjoy giving the above response. How far you go with it, of course, depends on your urgency factor. You would at least give them something to think about, although they might conclude that you were not really interested in the position.)

25. Are you analytical? Give an example.

"Yes. One Saturday morning I began thinking about how we handled work flow, and I laid out all the forms and steps that were necessary to move a job from the customer order through the warehouse to where it was ready to ship. My analysis showed how three steps and four forms could be eliminated. This enabled my boss to realign the work and saved him from hiring two additional people."

26. Are you creative? Give an example.

"Yes. I invented the Rabostat Upturner. You know that this is now the most profitable product at my company." (At this point in the question-and-answer session, you may be saying to yourself, "This guy wants me to tell him I'm perfect at everything. If I keep on answering everything this way, he's going to be sick. I've just bragged about how analytical I am, and now this char-

83

acter wants me to be creative as well." My response is to remind you that your goal is the job offer, and you will only lose points by trying to be subtle. Fight that urge to be humble. You are going through the Miss America process, so remember the words of Johnny Mercer if you don't want to be culled. Also, you are probably not going to be asked all fifty of these questions, nor will the questions come in such rapid-fire order. So go ahead and tell him how creative you really are.)

27. Are you a good worker? Give an example.

"I am known to be a careful worker. When key customer meetings are scheduled, I always get the job of handling the arrangements."

28. Are you a leader? Give an example.

"No. I generally like to work toward the goals set by someone else." (Fooled you on this one, but that answer is not a negative. There is a world shortage of good followers, and you will probably have determined by now that this is what the DM is after. Ultimately, you may decide that you don't want the job, but you do want to be in the position of getting an offer and having a choice.)

29. What is your personal net worth?

"I have equity in my house and car, and I have an IRA." (If you don't care about the job offer, say, "None of your business." If you do care, reply along the lines suggested.)

30. What are your feelings about divorce—or women in business, abortion, religion, etc.?

"My attitude is live and let live. I respect the rights of others and guard my own." (Tread lightly here. Your DM can have strong opinions on just about anything.)

31. Why do you think you will do well in this job?

"The work you want done is what I like to do and what I happen to be good at. As customer service manager at my present company, I have substantially reduced the number of serious customer complaints, that is, the ones that get to my management. If you have similar needs, I can certainly help."

32. What was the last book you read? The last movie, sporting event, or cultural event you attended?

"The last book I read was called *Get a Better Job!*" (Be careful with this one. The DM may have read, seen, or attended what you mention. It would be embarrassing to admit you fell asleep before the ending, only to discover that the DM was riveted to the seat.)

33. Are you talking to other companies? If so, which ones?

"I am not free to say. There are incumbents in the positions to be filled." (This question is out of line. What would happen if you asked for the names of the other people being interviewed?)

34. Give your concept of the job that we have open.

"I believe you are looking for an engineering manager who knows your present product line but can also direct the development of products for new markets." (Anticipate this question by finding out first what the DM considers the job to be. Early in the interview, say, "Your personnel department has done an excellent job of preparing me for this interview and describing the position that is open, but I would really like to have your thoughts about its important points." Then, when you are asked this question, you can parrot the DM's ideas back.)

35. What do you know about our company?

"You are one of the leading companies in the manufacture of industrial motors, and your name is a synonym for quality throughout the market. You do business of about $45-million a year and employ about 450 people. This year, you introduced a new line of fractional horsepower motors that has left the competition standing still." (If you cannot answer this one by the time you get to an interview with the primary or assistant DM, you have not been doing your homework.)

36. Why do you want to work for us?

"I want to work for your company because it offers a career path in which I can apply my skills to help you grow profitably. And that will mean a growth opportunity for me." (If you have decided you really don't want to work for this company, try answers like "It's close to home," "I hear you don't have to work very hard on the second shift," "My buddy in the Hell's Angels works here," or "I want to help bring in a union.")

37. What do you find most attractive in this position? Least attractive?

"The most attractive aspect of this job is that it fits both my background and what I like to do and do well. I wish the new computer system were already here, but I guess I can wait the three months until it is delivered." (The latter is a not very negative negative.)

38. How long have you been looking for new employment?

"I started my search two weeks ago." (State the truth in whatever way you want, as long as it doesn't indicate that you have been out of work for a long time. If you win the job offer, the amount of money tied to it will be affected by the length of time you have been "on the beach." If they think you are "hungry," they will tend to offer less money.)

39. What position do you expect to have in five years?

"I am very impressed by your operation and the job you want done. I would hope that I can do the job well enough to some-day follow in your footsteps." (As already mentioned, one of the pitfalls in interviewing is to come across as a threat to the DM, creating the fear that hiring you might eventually push him or her out of a job. More on this later. For now, think about a wrong answer like "I would expect to be a vice president within five years." If you say this to a DM who is still hoping to get his or her name on a parking space after ten years' service and is nowhere near a vice presidency, you have just become a threat. You will be pictured leaving footprints up the back of everyone between your present desk and the front office. The DM will take no chances, and you will be brushed off with one of the old standbys, such as "You are obviously very talented and capable. Too bad you are overqualified.")

40. Do you feel that you have supervisory potential? Why?

"No. I'm an individual contributor and am not interested in supervisory work." (Nothing negative about this if you have figured out that it's what the DM wants. On the other hand, if you sense that the job requires supervisory skills, you might reply, "Yes. Right now I direct the efforts of three people in shipping, and the boss always puts me in charge of the department when he is away.")

41. How long would you stay with our company?

"I want this to be my permanent career spot." (Whenever the question comes up, which it does often and in many forms, this is always the right answer.)

42. What important trends do you see in our industry?

"I see great growth in the field in the immediate future, and that's exactly why I am so interested in joining your company now."

43. Do you feel that you might be better off in a company of a different size?

"I am contemplating an important career move. I am not looking for just another job, and I would not be here if I did not feel this was the right company of the right size for me."

44. Do you think that you may be overqualified for this position?

"I am good at my job, as evidenced by my performance at Mega Pharmaceuticals, but I know I have much to learn before I'm at the top of my profession. Your opening offers that learning opportunity, and I am in no way overqualified." (Of course, if you don't really want the job, you can always admit that you exaggerated on your resume and that you just seem to be overqualified when in reality you can barely hack it.)

45. I've been told you pay more attention to discotheques than business when you're traveling. Is that true?

"I imagine if you asked around enough you could hear anything you liked about me. I like a good time as much as anyone, but the important thing is that I get the job done, whether at home or on a three-week trip." (Reputation questions come in all forms: "Would you say your reputation for cleaning house by firing people and then bringing in your own is justified?" "Is it true that you are quite the playboy?" "You did not do well in college. How come?" These can be some of the toughest questions to handle, because they concern you personally and are usually based on rumor. A trusted friend can be helpful in finding out what rumbles on the grapevine about you, but don't make a big thing out of what you hear. Give a brief answer to the DM's question and then go offstage. Drop it. The worst thing you can do is try to explain, justify your actions, or protest. Brush the question off as you would a bothersome mosquito.)

SPECIAL OPPORTUNITY QUESTIONS

The following questions deserve special treatment. They offer the greatest opportunity to be negative and "step in your own mess kit," so I am giving them particular emphasis.

46. Why are you leaving your present job? Why did you leave the job before that? Before that?

"It is my feeling that I have accomplished all I can in my present job and it is time to move on. My boss agrees and has played an important role in helping me make this decision."

When asked your reasons for leaving, it may seem the logical thing to mention that the management was dishonest and wanted you to engage in unethical conduct, your boss had personal problems and was impossible to work for, you found it necessary to sue the company for unfair employment practices, the company was anti-union, or quality control was exceedingly poor. These are all valid reasons for leaving a job. Never use them. They are negative and prompt negative reactions. Did you contribute to your boss's personal problems? Are you calling the management dishonest to cover up your own dishonesty? Was the company simply a tough competitor, not unethical? Aren't people who sue always troublemakers? Was the union perhaps unreasonable? Why didn't you try to improve quality?

For each job you have had you must have an honest and positive reason for leaving. It should be accurate and uncontroversial. If you give reasons that sound critical, you will be suspected of being part of the problem. Furthermore, the DM will wonder what you'd be saying after you left his or her company.

YOU MUST HAVE A POSITIVE REASON FOR LEAVING
EACH JOB.

When you dig deeply enough, you can find a reason that is also true. Tim Zane was fired. He had been based in St. Louis as district sales manager for a large chemical company. He explained his firing as follows: "I was chosen to be master of ceremonies at our western sales conference, and I told some jokes in an attempt to loosen up the audience. The next week I was let go because the jokes I told were said to be in poor taste."

I counseled Tim that he had to do better. If he had been valuable in his district, the most he would have gotten was a mild reprimand from his boss. Tim should and could have come up with something that was both true and positive, such as: "My job was to sell a product line that was still in the developmental stage, and there was not much opportunity to earn incentive pay. I also felt I had run my course at Carlson Ceramics, so I sat down with my boss and we both agreed I should leave."

This is a nice, innocuous statement that is also true. It has nothing negative about it. The DM may or may not check with Carlson Ceramics, but no one will ever be blamed for telling the truth.

In response to the question of why she left her last job, Jennifer Rhodes replies, "My boss and I sat down to discuss my career, and we agreed that I was logjammed in my job and should find an open pathway. He was very complimentary and has been very helpful."

Ralph Miller says, "It looks to me like the new owners of my company are going to install their own management. That has been their history with acquisitions. I think it is wise for me to look for new pastures."

John Allard answers, "I've enjoyed running my own company but have had to be on duty seven days a week. My wife and I agree that it is time to take our winnings and get back to a more structured life, so I am selling the business."

Lynn Longmyer says, "I have started a family, and now it is time to get back to my career."

My purpose here is to convince you to prepare positive responses to the question of why you left your job. They should be well thought out and written down on index cards, one for each company you have worked for. You should study these responses and be prepared to deliver them by rote.

47. Do you drink?

"Yes, I do." (This is one of those times when a simple "yes" or "no" is best. If you are next asked how much you drink, avoid flip answers, such as "Less than a fifth a day," and make it clear that you partake only socially. If you should happen to have a problem, don't pick the interview as a place to discuss it.)

48. Do you take drugs?

"No, I don't." (You may be asked if you are willing to undergo drugs testing. Decide your position ahead of time, tempering your answer according to how much you want the job.)

49. How much money do you want?

"The important thing to me now is career path. This is a reasonable company, and I know you will make me a reasonable offer." (Never answer this question with a figure! Chapter 14 is devoted to salary negotiations. Until then, add this message to the one already written in your hat: "Never answer the question 'How much money do you want?'" To answer with a specific amount is to risk pricing yourself out of the competition or leaving money on the table.)

50. Will you be out to take your boss's job?

"I'm very interested in the position we have talked about, and I know I am the person for the job. I am good at what I do but also know that I need more experience and training. I feel I would get this under you, and I hope that you would keep your eye on me for possible promotion as you move up the line." (This may seem like a rather innocuous question designed to test whether you are ambitious or not, but be careful. Business literature reports a surprising incidence of management insecurity. The last thing a Decision Maker wants is to hire someone who will push him or her aside. The example given expresses reasonable ambition while offering no threat.)

The Value of Positive Action

A good part of this chapter has been spent on detailed discussion of the fifty "opportunity questions." This was to make sure that you apply a very positive, self-serving strategy to your pursuit of a new job. Don't be upset by the term "self-serving." You are after a good job, the job of your choice. As you strive toward this goal, ask, "If I don't serve myself, who will?" And remember that the Decision Makers will be strictly self-serving as they select the winning candidates. What's fair is fair. Remember:

> *You've got to Ac-cent-tchu-ate The Positive,*
> *E-lim-my-nate the negative,*
> *Latch on to the affirmative,*
> *Don't mess with Mister Inbetween.*

Show your good side, cover your bruises, and become the winning tomato. Up until this point, the DM has had all the options, but once you have the offer in your hand, the ball is in your court. This is what you are working toward.

The Decision Maker's Code

You have now arrived at what will become the most valuable item in your collection of job-search treasures, the gem that will set you off from the others. Make it the bedrock on which your new-job campaign is based.

Before I hand over this treasure, consider a typical position guide. This one was written by a Decision Maker who was starting a new organization to develop products for the architectural market.

POSITION GUIDE

Position Title
Program/Engineering Manager
Reports to
General Manager

Purpose of Position
The individual will be responsible for managing all of the technical
and engineering activities related to the application of advanced
materials to architectural markets. He or she will interface with the
customer to establish project requirements. This individual will
then take these requirements and direct internal programs to develop the necessary products.

Knowledge and Experience
The individual must have a thorough knowledge of CAD/CAM. He
or she must have had experience in structural analysis using advanced materials and must have demonstrated the ability to identify requirements and establish good working relationships with
customers. The individual must also have a degree in mechanical
engineering or structural analysis.

Principal Responsibilities
Managing and directing the technical applications and develop-
ment activities for advanced materials in the architectural market.
Creating the design strategy.
Managing technical resources within the department and coordi-
nating these with the business plan.
Managing internal functional resources.
Creating a design that is of the highest quality, cost-competitive,
and producible.

This position guide lists many important criteria for picking the
successful candidate, but it leaves out the most important one. It
fails to take into account the "Decision Maker's code." There
should be another category for "Most Important Ability Required,"
and in it should be:

TO MAKE THE DECISION MAKER LOOK GOOD.

Now you have it: the criterion that will be used to make the final
choice. The DM will wonder, "Which one of these finalists is going
to do the best job of making me look good?" This ultimate standard
strips away all the fancy words of ads, position guides, letters, and
resumes. It boils down all the questioning, evaluating, and sparring
to the essence of the hiring decision. The Decision Maker's code is
to *hire the one who will do the best job of making the DM look good.*
This code is unwritten. You will not find it in the rules and

regulations, textbooks, management treatises, personnel practices manuals, or position guides, not even in a DM's penciled notes. Nonetheless, it is applied in every case.

Don't judge Decision Makers too harshly for wanting to look good. They are like all the rest of us. They follow their natural instinct, which is to succeed. And, unless you're a hermit, looking good is essential to success.

As the DM applies the code, he or she will consider, at least subliminally, such ego-oriented questions as these:

"If I hire this accountant, will she help me get a handle on the cost overruns?"

"Will this pilot improve my on-time and safety records?"

"Can this quality control manager cut my scrap rate and get the boss off my back?"

"Is this the food chemist who can give me the new products I need to meet the company's growth objectives?"

I suspect that the majority of Decision Makers do not even realize that they apply such a code. And I suspect that those who do won't admit it. Whichever is the case, knowing this criterion will put you ahead of the pack. In Chapter 12, you will learn how to capitalize on this knowledge at the interview, and in Chapter 20, you will discover ways of applying it at your new job. For now, just think about all the implications of this newfound knowledge for your job search.

Chapter 8

Rejection and Depression

"Trying to conduct a job campaign while depressed is like trying to run the 100-yard dash in 2 feet of water. Happily there is no need to."

You know how to set your new job objectives, you are prepared to use the tools and pathways, and you understand the selection process. You are now ready to charge ahead and captivate those Decision Makers. Right? Wrong!

The Weather Along Your Route

A summer flight from Patrick Air Force Base across the Florida peninsula to MacDill Air Force Base at Tampa is bound to encounter a squall line of cumulonimbus clouds. When I was flying, we used to call these thunderclouds "cumulobumpus." They are beasts to go through and best avoided. A weather check will tell the pilot what detour to take or the route of least turbulence.

Before taking off on your job campaign, you too should check the weather ahead. The forecast will undoubtedly include "some rejection along all pathways." And just as running into a thunderstorm can delay your flight, running into rejection on the road to a new job can hamper your efforts to get offers.

Some pilots can handle thunderstorms with greater tranquility than others, and some of us can experience rejection with little or no adverse effects. This chapter is directed to those of you who have difficulty coping when rebuffed. But the rest of you hang in here. The medicine is not bitter and may just prove valuable to you (despite your thick skin).

Thunderstorms are at their most threatening when a lack of

pilot skill allows them to endanger the aircraft. Rejection becomes harmful when you allow the experience to result in depression. This suggests the major connection between rejection and depression—you!

Record Your Rejections

Before we go any further, please perform the following exercise. On one side of a sheet of paper, record the five most serious rejections you have experienced in your lifetime. As you did with your list of accomplishments during the goal-setting work, mull over your list of rejections at leisure so that you arrive at the most significant ones. Fold the sheet in half. Staple it closed and put it in a safe place. You will retrieve it later.

The Process of Rejection and Depression

As you proceed along your course to captivate those DMs, employing the tools and following the pathways, rejections will come from all directions. With advance warning, you can avoid many rejections and learn to handle the rest.

Rejections come in many types:

"Sorry, she is in conference."

"Sorry, no mail for you today."

"We found your background to be very interesting but have no position for you in our organization at this time. We will keep your resume on file."

"I realize that you have called three times, but Mr. Wright is a very busy man. I'll tell him you called again."

"Your qualifications are excellent, and everyone who interviewed you liked you very much. However, we have decided to offer the position to a candidate who has more experience in interior design."

"Your qualifications are excellent, but frankly you are overqualified." (You're too old.)

"Your background is outstanding, but we need someone with more experience." (You're too young.)

"You interviewed very well, but we do not feel that you would be a good fit with the group." (The DM didn't like the way you combed your hair; you went to the wrong college; you were in the wrong branch of the service.)

These are just a few of the forms that rejection can and will take. So what? We know they are in our path. Knowing they are there, we can avoid them or roll with them, and the effectiveness of our campaign will not be blunted.

"To reject" means to refuse to accept, consider, recognize, or submit to; to discard as useless or unsatisfactory; and to cast out or eject. A "reject" is an imperfect article. Rejection is an entirely negative notion.

And depression? When they're depressed, people feel as if they are and always will be "losers" (of jobs, friends, self-esteem, etc.). They believe their efforts are bound to fail, so the future looks bleak and devoid of prospects for satisfaction and achievement. They have no motivation to set goals and feel sad, passive, and guilty. Even the positive things that happen are discounted or denied. Hardly the frame of mind for a new-job campaign, is it? Trying to conduct a job campaign while depressed is like trying to run the 100-yard dash in 2 feet of water. Happily there is no need to.

It was suggested earlier that *you* provide the major link between rejection and depression. Rejection becomes a problem only when you let it result in depression. Rejection results in depression through the so-called ABC method of cognition.

A is the stimulus.
C is the emotional response.
B is the blank between A and C that is filled
   by automatic thoughts.

This process seems to be a "closed-loop system," in that once the stimulus has occurred, things proceed to the emotional response as a matter of course. In the case of rejection, the automatic thought process results in depression, as in the following example:

A (stimulus): Losing your job.
B (automatic thought): "I'm a failure."
C (emotion): Sadness, anger, depression.

Between stimulus A and emotion C, thought B jumps in, seemingly automatically: "I'm no good," "Nobody will like me," "Nobody will hire me," "I will never get a good job," "I'll never be happy again," "I am just plain unemployable!" Depression rushes in.

This discussion of depression would be misleading without the inclusion of a disclaimer. My intent is to alert you to the depressions that result from specific situations, in particular the job search. There is no attempt here to analyze or even discuss serious emotional disturbances that require clinical treatment. They are not only beyond the scope of this book but also beyond my ability to make any meaningful contribution.

Handling Rejection

We can foil many rejections by avoiding them. We can slough many off by anticipating them. For the rest, we must handle them by introducing a glitch in the automatic thinking process, that seemingly spontaneous routine that compels us to translate rejection into depression. The point is,

---

YOU ARE IN CHARGE. YOU CONTROL THE
THOUGHT LINK BETWEEN REJECTION AND
DEPRESSION.

Here is a simple example of avoiding the kind of setup in which rejections can occur. I always feel a tinge of resentment when the efficient-sounding secretary asks, "Who is calling, please?" It suggests to me that I may not be the right person and will flunk some sort of screening. I avoid this possibility by always saying something like this: "Is Mr. Potentate in? This is Ed Rushlow calling." In doing so, I not only deprive the secretary of an opportunity to reject me, but I also put him or her on the alert that this call is *different.* Secretaries always ask, "Who is calling?" and this breaks the routine. The secretary may not catch your name and will have to ask, giving you a point in the game of one-upmanship.

There are many subtle points like this that will minimize your exposure to rejection, but your basic approach should be to use the tools and pathways as you have learned. The best way to neutralize the rejections that do get through is to remind yourself that *you* allow them to result in depression and *you* can prevent this from happening. It is also helpful to realize that at least 95 percent of the rejections you will meet are impersonal. This is worthy of repetition.

AT LEAST 95 PERCENT OF THE REJECTIONS YOU WILL MEET ARE IMPERSONAL.

Consider telephone rejections. "Who is calling, please?" "He is in conference." "Ms. Fullbright asked that I return your call. She has no opening for a person of your qualifications." To the rejecter on the telephone, you are nothing but a phone number or a resume. How impersonal can you get? When you answer ads and get nothing but "Dear Johns" or no answers at all, that too is highly impersonal. Pieces of paper have been rejected, not you. When your letter campaign gets no results, that is not personal rejection either. It simply means that your letters did not meet with a need for your talents.

Unfortunately, in my business it is necessary for me to reject an average of fifteen resumes a week out of the large numbers that are always arriving. All come with glowing covering letters expounding the excellence of their authors. It takes about 3 seconds to determine whether a particular candidate fits the needs of any of my clients. I am being highly impersonal. So is the ad culler who rejects 735 out of 740 responses.

When your proposal of marriage is turned down, that's personal. When you are sued for divorce, that's even more personal. When, after three rounds of interviews, you are told the other candidate got the job, that is also highly personal. This is when you need to step in and block the automatic thought link between rejection and the depression that can destroy the effectiveness of your job search. Try to remember that you can't win them all.

So What?

Now it's time to retrieve the paper on which you wrote your five worst rejections. If you're a speed-reader and you charged ahead without doing the exercise, please do it now. If you're a procrastinator and you thought you'd do the exercise later, the time has come. Put the book down, describe your five most serious rejections on a sheet of paper, fold it and staple it closed, and come back tomorrow. No peeking ahead.

The rest of us will forge ahead right now. Do not open the paper. Instead, with a big, red, felt-tip pen, write on the outside "SO WHAT!"

Ask yourself, "What did those rejections really amount to, anyway?" In the first place, you had to think long and hard to come up with five. In the second, you probably can't recall all the ones you did choose without sneaking a look. And in the third place, when you cut out the truly personal ones, none of them meant much anyway.

<hr>

SO YOU WERE REJECTED . . . SO WHAT!

<hr>

Complete the exercise by deep-sixing your list without opening it. You are now rid of those rejections forever. Future ones can be painlessly deflected, and depression can be defeated. Isn't knowledge wonderful!

About this time you may be saying, "What's the big deal about rejection and depression? With me rejection and depression don't amount to a sneeze in a whirlwind." Great. That's just how I want you to feel, and if it takes a little overkill to get you to say that and believe it, I'm happy.

The Case of Al Perry

Consider Al Perry. He had been manager of production for a printing company that was acquired and merged into a similar operation by its new owners. As a result of the merger, there were two heads of production, and Al, being the acquiree, was the one to go. This was a rejection on the basis of circumstance and not personality. Al felt no depression, particularly because he was offered a generous "golden handshake" (six months' severance pay, with full benefits and outplacement). But Al made some mistakes. The first one was taking an additional cash settlement in lieu of outplacement. The second was buying a motor home so that he and his wife could spend the next nine months seeing the country. And his third mistake was assuming that he would be able to find his next position as soon as he threw the switch.

When Al did start his new-job campaign, he found that the road was rougher than he had anticipated. Just like the rest of us, he ran into bad weather in the form of rejection. His savings dwindled as the "Dear Johns" piled up. He denied that he was depressed or ever could be. He described the fine offers (real or imagined) he was about to receive and talked about how difficult it was going to be to make a choice.

Believe me, Al had become depressed. You could read it in the set of his jaw. (Press the hinge of your jaw between your thumb and middle finger . . . that's where depression shows. Of course, you can't go around squeezing jaws. Just look.) But Al evaluated his situation and shook his depression when he understood that he was in control. Then he was free to really begin working with the tools and pathways. At this writing, he did indeed have two fine offers, and his jaw was relaxed.

Jim Kramer's Depression

Unlike Al Perry, Jim Kramer was rejected in a personal sense. The reason he gave for leaving his last job was "management disagreement," but he had been fired. Analysis revealed that Jim forgot he was there to make the Decision Maker look good. Worse than that, he got into a power struggle with the DM, his boss, which was equivalent to bringing the guillotine down on his own neck.

Jim was offered outplacement, and he took it. This meant that his former company salved its conscience and contracted, on Jim's behalf (and at a cost of from 12 to 15 percent of Jim's annual salary), with a firm that specialized in counseling displaced employees in the work of finding new jobs. Outplacement is described in detail in Chapter 6. For Jim Kramer, it provided an office that appeared to be his place of employment, plus telephone coverage and the clerical help he needed to conduct an effective job search.

So how do I know Jim Kramer was depressed? Only because I have been there. Jim was not making use of the outplacement service. He was not sending out letters or answering ads. Sometimes it took him three days to answer calls made to his "office." Jim had given up; he probably was convinced that he was unemployable. The ABC pattern of thought had done its work. Jim was waiting for whatever job came along, and that's exactly what he finally landed, but not without a lot of help from an expert contingency recruiter who saw a chance for a bounty.

Fall and Rise of a VP

It was a Friday, and the vodka was flowing as Flight 117 played along the jetstream. The captain had given the customary assurances that the flight was making the expected progress toward Headquarters City. On board were the division president and his vice president of marketing, relaxing after a tough week with the subassembly department in Outpost City.

Not only the vodka was flowing. The division president showered Mr. VP with praise for his fine work during the week and since joining the company. Mr. VP could not help but bask a bit in the praise.

The following Tuesday, Mr. VP was fired by the same boss who had praised him the week before. It was obvious there had been orders from above. The vice president fell into deep depression, victim of the infamous ABCs:

A (stimulus): Mr. VP was fired, a serious personal rejection.
B (thought process): "I am a failure. I am no good. Nobody likes me. I will never get another job. I am unemployable."
C (emotion): For several months, insidious depression took its toll on Mr. VP.

In spite of a very generous "golden handshake" that included a year's salary with full benefits and his company car, Mr. VP was depressed, although he would not or could not recognize it. Like a reluctant door-to-door salesman who hopes no one is at home, he began to avoid opportunities for further rejection. Naturally his job search efforts were ineffectual.

The depression eventually drained away, and Mr. VP went on to become the president of a growing computer services company. It took him ten years to understand what had happened. He finally realized that he had been fired not because he was inadequate at his job but because his performance level was too high. As he looked back, he was able to trace a pattern of dismissals similar to his. The higher-up who had ordered him fired had done the same to two other VPs who were conspicuous performers—this executive was taking no chances on having people around him who might take his job. Rather than a personal rejection, Mr. VP's firing was a recognition of his ability.

This had been a costly lesson to learn, since before Mr. VP shook off the depression and began working at his new-job campaign, the "golden handshake" had expired, and he was consuming his savings. If he had understood earlier what he realized ten years later, Mr. VP would not have sunk into the quagmire of depression. And even without this important understanding, he might have avoided bogging down if he had been able to recognize the automatic thought process that had gone on and the fact that he was actually in control.

The Last Word on Rejection

Maybe you have just been rejected by being fired or acquired, replaced or displaced, declared useless or surplus. As you proceed in your job search, you will receive many more rejections. Letters will not be answered. Calls will not be returned. There will be no results from your answers to ads. Decision Makers will keep you waiting 45 minutes while they do something that is obviously more important to them than interviewing you. You will be shuffled off to the personnel office. Your interviews will be interrupted by bosses, secretaries, spouses, and assorted hangers-on. And then another candidate will get the offer.

Don't think you can mount your white stallion and charge off to conquer rejection. You must realize that, in any job search, there is rejection ahead that can result in depression. Some rejections can be anticipated and avoided by the informed use of the tools and pathways. Most rejections are impersonal and of no consequence. Those that *are* personal can be handled by:

- Acknowledging that no one wins all the time.
- Saying "So what!" It means little in the long run.
- Understanding the process that leads to depression and knowing that you're in control.

You Can Be Happy

The idea that *you* are the link between rejection and depression is encapsulated in the words of the Roger Miller song, "You Can't Roller Skate in a Buffalo Herd":

Well, you can't roller skate in a buffalo herd,
You can't roller skate in a buffalo herd,
You can't roller skate in a buffalo herd,
But you can be happy if you've a mind to.

You can't take a shower in a parakeet cage,
You can't take a shower in a parakeet cage,
You can't take a shower in a parakeet cage,
But you can be happy if you've a mind to.

All you gotta do is put your mind to it,
Knuckle down, buckle down, do it, do it, do it!

You can't go swimming in a baseball pool,
You can't go swimming in a baseball pool,
You can't go swimming in a baseball pool,
But you can be happy if you've a mind to.

. . . .

All you gotta do is put your mind to it,
Knuckle down, buckle down, do it, do it, do it!

If this wisdom is applied to the problems of job search, a new verse emerges that goes like this:

> *You can't be sharp if you're depressed,*
> *You can't be sharp if you're depressed,*
> *You can't be sharp if you're depressed,*
> *But you can be right on if you've a mind to.*
>
> *All you gotta do is put your mind to it,*
> *Knuckle down, buckle down, do it, do it, do it!*

Chapter 9

Telephone Style

"Skillful use of the telephone will speed you toward the in-person interview with the Decision Maker."

A National Football League coach was quoted as saying to his team, "I really don't care what kind of a dance you guys do in the end zone. Just be sure you act like you've been there before." The same is true when you are on the telephone: you have to act like you've been there before. This is easy to do. All it takes are a few simple procedures. With my apologies to the authors Strunk and White, I am going to give you "The Elements of Style" for reaching out by telephone.

Having a professional telephone style is important to me because almost all my work as a headhunter is done by phone. (The saying in my trade is, "If you are not on the phone, you are unemployed.") Good phone style is of similar importance to your job search, because you aren't going to earn a choice of new jobs without spending important time communicating by telephone. Skillful use of the telephone will speed you toward the in-person interview with the Decision Maker.

Ma Bell and her competitors will help you to:

- Uncover job openings.
- Gather information about targeted companies.
- Reach Decision Makers.
- Obtain interviews.
- Earn job offers.

And on the road to an offer, it is highly likely that you also will be subjected to an interview over the phone. (The telephone interview can be a critical event, and it is given special attention in Chapter 11.)

A Primer of Style

Good telephone style does not mean canned presentations like those used by telemarketers to present bargains in Florida swampland or $399 prearranged funerals. It does mean neat procedures that work. Here is the way I conduct a call:

"Northwest Escalators."

"Hi, Northwest. I'm calling to talk to Ms. August."

"One moment, I will connect you."

. . . .

"Ms. August's office, can I help you?"

"Hi. Is Ms. August in? This is Ed Rushlow calling from Florida."

"She is in a meeting. May I have her call you?"

"Please do. My first name is Ed, and my last name is Rushlow, spelled R-U-S-H-L-O-W. My number is 904-555-6451, and Jean will know why I'm calling."

Sounds simple enough, but there are some intricacies. Notice that I said, "Hi, Northwest," to the operator. Some progressive companies have the operators tell you their name: "Northwest Escalators, Evelyn speaking." In this case, my greeting becomes, "Hi, Evelyn." Phone operators appreciate being treated as individuals and show their appreciation by making an extra effort. They can be very helpful in giving you information, identifying the right person to speak to, locating that person in the building, and so on.

When I get through to my party's office, it is always "This is Ed Rushlow calling from Florida." This routine averts the standard "Who's calling, please?" or the more polite "Can I tell her who's calling?" To me, these questions always imply that I may not be important enough to get through, and I like to avoid them. Announcing that I am calling from Florida means the call will be taken more seriously, since it is usually long-distance. There is no reason why this should be so in our communicating society, but it is. Besides, this fact provides the secretary with some information to give the boss, and, like everyone else, the secretary enjoys being knowledgeable and needed.

Always answer "yes" to the question "Shall I have her call you?" This is not only so you will talk on the company's nickel, though that does help. The main reason is because it gives you the option play. You can always call back if you wish, but you are ahead of the game if the party calls you. Another advantage is that the conversation will take place at the caller's convenience, and you will have a more receptive audience as a result.

Always spell your name (even if it is J-O-N-E-S) and give your phone number distinctly. One of the important tasks of the person answering the phone is to report these facts accurately, and their tone of voice will convey appreciation for your thoughtfulness.

Always use the first name of the person you're calling (if you're sure of it) and say, for example, "Jean will know why I'm calling," whenever there is the slightest possibility that this is true. In my work, I use some form of this phrase about 90 percent of the time, taking the attitude that *everyone* knows I am a recruiter. If you feel bold, you can take the position that your party will know why you are calling just as soon as you get on the line and disclose the reason.

Cold Calls

Cold-calling means that you select a company, identify the appropriate Decision Maker, and call to request an interview. Some job seekers I have counseled have been comfortable with the cold call, but I have always preferred to precede the call with a letter. My theory is this: a phone call is not going to create a hiring need if one does not exist. A written presentation, however, can plant the idea in the organization that it might need a person like you. Then when you follow up by phone and are asked, "Can I tell him why you are calling?" you can answer by mentioning your letter. The secretary will remember the letter and may even dig it out for the DM to refer to. Of course, if an opening already exists and the letter has been circulated to the interested parties, you have two strings to your bow. If you hit either target, you will get an interview.

Here is how Jennifer Rhodes makes a cold call to a target Decision Maker without first sending a letter:

"Hello, this is Daniels Dental Supply."

"Hi, Daniels. I'm calling for Rhoda Williams."

"One moment please."

. . . .

"Ms. Williams's office. Helga speaking."

"Hello, Helga. Is Ms. Williams in? This is Jennifer Rhodes calling from Los Angeles."

"I'm sorry, she is with a client. May I have her call you?"

"Please do. My first name is Jennifer, and my last name is Rhodes, R-H-O-D-E-S. My phone number is 213-555-3785."

At this point, Jennifer knows that the next question will be about her reason for calling. She can say, "Rhoda will know why I am calling" (just as soon as Jennifer tells her), say that it is a personal matter, or simply explain her reason. There is no need to lie or be defensive, so Jennifer's choice is to give her reason. She gives Helga plenty of detail, since a reason will be necessary eventually:

"Helga, I'm a senior buyer in jewelry at Madison's Department Store. You may be familiar with some of the lines I handle. Bronee, Elgard, and Frazee are among them. I'm interested in a career change and have called Ms. Williams to explore the possibility of a sales job with your company. I have a background in dentistry and have four years' experience in selling. It was my performance in sales that earned me the senior buyer position."

Now Helga has helpful details to give her boss, and if Rhoda is considering adding to her sales force she will return Jennifer's call.

A polished telephone style is a great asset, but the fact remains that if the person at the other end of the line does not want to talk to you or put you through to your party, there is nothing clever you can do. Be happy and go on to the next possibility.

Ralph Miller has learned that Acme Office Equipment may be looking for a new general manager. Here is the call he makes to research his target:

"Good morning. This is Acme Office Equipment."

"Hello, Acme. I would like to talk to someone in sales, please."

"One moment please."

. . . .

"Sales. Marge speaking. May I help you?"

"Marge, this is Ralph Miller. I'd like to talk to a salesperson."

"Which product are you interested in, Mr. Miller?"

"I'm interested in your steel desk line."

"Ms. Shenk can help you. I'll connect you."

. . . .

"Hello, Mr. Miller, this is Gloria Shenk. I'm Sales Manager for our steel products."

"Ms. Shenk, I'm calling to learn more about your company and its products. I am submitting my resume so that I will be considered for employment. I asked to talk to you because I felt you would be the best one to help me."

"We don't have any openings in sales."

"In fact, I'm not thinking about sales. My background is administrative. Who is your General Manager?"

"Gerry Morgan is, but I understand that he is moving up. He is probably still the right one to talk to about administrative work, though."

"Where can I see some of Acme's products?"

"We have a showroom at the warehouse on 32nd Street."

"Who is your main competitor?" (Other relevant questions would include "Why is your product better?" "Is this a good year for office equipment?" "What kind of manager is Mr. Morgan? Is he an engineer?" and so on.)

Ms. Shenk will no doubt be pleased to have the opportunity to tout her company and its products. My experience shows that most people are. Ralph will gain much valuable information that will help him zero in on his target. If Gloria Shenk does not tell him what he wants to know, he can keep calling until he finds someone who will.

Unlimited Opportunities

Your use of the telephone to gather information is limited only by your imagination. Remember how a phone call boosted me on the way to becoming president of that South Florida company by giving me information that helped me win an interview. Recall how, while others were composing their answers to the Singapore joint venture ad, I was already talking to the Decision Maker.

Here are some more ways of using the telephone that will help you to reach Decision Makers, win in-person interviews, and earn job offers:

- Call your friendly reference librarian. He or she will have a wealth of knowledge about information sources.
- Call the competitors of your targeted company to learn more about its product line and reputation.
- If you can find a former employee of your targeted company, you will gather all kinds of useful information . . . though you may want to disregard some of it, particularly if the parting was bitter.
- Call your broker and give the firm a chance to earn all those commissions you have paid. Most of what you want to know can be called up on the computer. The broker also can send you tear sheets from *Standard & Poor's Corporation Records,* a source of data on over 3,500 companies. The call won't cost you anything if you use the toll-free number, and your broker will be glad to help. If you have a better job, he or she might be able to sell you more stocks.
- Call the pertinent trade association. You will get glowing reports on any member company, a pitch urging you to join up, and just maybe some information of value, such as the results of a recent industry survey or a market forecast. (The local Better Business Bureau is similar, but even less critical.) While on the phone, you might as well ask for a roster of members, but don't try to reach them all. Remember, rifle shot, rifle shot, rifle shot!

Transmission Blocks and Counterblocks

Face the facts. If the person you are calling doesn't want to talk to you, there is nothing you can do. If a secretary wants to block you, getting through will be like trying to get the maitre d' to give you a choice table for a Las Vegas show without flashing a $10 bill. There is no way.

But don't make a big deal of this. I have to think back many years to recall an incident where I received an outright refusal. On that occasion, I had called Mr. Importance for a lead on a candidate to fill a top management position. His secretary, Ms. Barrier, seemed to have the single mission in life of preventing anyone from talking to her boss. My statement, "Bruce will know why I'm calling," did not fly. She demanded details, which I gave her: "I am a recruiter on the search for a key executive, and I believe Mr. Importance could recommend a candidate." Her response was, "Mr. Importance does not talk to recruiters," and the line went dead. I felt sorry for Mr. Importance, who had been deprived of valuable information on an open executive position and general news about the top-management employment picture. Besides, he had a very rude secretary.

I've always had the urge (after the fact) to play dirty with a Ms. or Mr. Barrier. If you know you are going to be blocked, maybe you can vent some frustration with one of these answers to the "Why are you calling?" question:

"I'm investigating some matters for the IRS."

"I'm calling about those gambling debts."

"I think I just backed into your boss's Mercedes."

Just be sure that you leave a wrong number, hang up when your call is returned, or are skilled at handling mad dogs. But this probably won't be a problem if, like me, you are ready to street fight only after you have hung up.

You've heard about the absolute barrier I encountered. In addition to secretaries like Ms. Barrier, switchboard operators, personnel departments, and the Decision Makers themselves can place obstacles in your way. With the good telephone style you are learning here you will be able to prevent them from becoming anything more than nuisances. Dealing with personnel departments is discussed in detail in the next chapter.

Switchboard Operators

There are three types of operator. The first is knowledgeable and helpful and will speed you on your way to the Decision Maker. The second would like to help but does not have the required information. The third is trained to filter out all calls not made to a person by name. This type will try to brush you off with statements like "I'm sorry, I cannot connect you with just 'anyone in engineering.' I must have a name," or "No, I cannot give you the name of the Manager of Accounting. It's company policy not to give out names."

Most of the time, you will talk to a helpful operator. You will simply ask for the information you need and get it.

"Who is the Manager of Manufacturing?"

"Who is responsible for bookkeeping?"

"Who is your First Shift Foreman?"

The second type of operator calls for a more roundabout approach:

"Please let me talk to the secretary in Manufacturing."

"Please let me talk to someone in Accounting."

"Could you connect me with Sales, please?"

It is the third case that can be troublesome. We headhunters feel that operators are trained to filter out calls not placed to particular staff members primarily to make it more difficult for us to steal people. Another theory is that this practice makes it possible to divert job hunters to the personnel office. Also, it can be because the company does not want unauthorized sources leaking information to unauthorized recipients. IBM is a good example. I have always found that its switchboard operators are trained not to put you through without a specific name.

However, there is always a new bullet invented to pierce the newest bulletproof vest. With companies like IBM, you can get the desired information, a name that will get you beyond the switchboard, by doing some or all of the following:

- Reading their house organ.
- Reading the local newspaper.
- Reading the names on parking spaces at the company's offices.
- Reading license plates. (Proper courtesy extended to a local law enforcement officer can translate a registration number into a name. Just kidding, honest.)

How far you carry this depends on how strongly you feel about getting where you want to go.

Secretaries

Again, there are three classes of secretary. There is the communicator who makes sure the boss is open to all opportunities, usually on the boss's own instructions. The second kind is a robot who asks, "Who is calling?" "What is this about?" etc. This person doesn't really care about the answer but has been programmed by someone who really didn't care either. And then there is the one who has taken the obstructionist oath never to let anyone talk to the boss a first time or any other time. This one has a full arsenal of weapons, including these:

"She is not in the office" (with no offer to help).

"He is in conference" (with no offer to help).

"He is out of town for a week" (with no offer to help).

"What company are you with?"

"Is this about employment? Send a resume."

"Is this about employment? Call Personnel."

The secretary and boss of the first type make the world a much better place to work in, at the same time enhancing their own professional standing. The second type of secretary presents no problem. Give your name and company and any subject you think will interest the boss.

There is no doubt the third category can be troublesome. Ray Beddingfield of Colorado Springs, top executive-search specialist and my mentor in the recruiting business, gave these secretaries a title: saber-toothed tigers. I've already given you advice on how to get around the tiger.

"It's a personal call."

"He'll know why I'm calling."

"She is expecting my call."

But the tiger has all the moves, and if that tiger is dedicated to keeping the obstructionist oath, you don't have a chance. The only way around then is to convince the tiger that the boss will lose by not talking to you and will blame the one who refused to let you through.

Imagine a scene in which John Allard has called to talk to the Manager of Advertising of Eye-Ease Optical. None of his ploys has worked, and the saber-toothed tiger is about to hang up on him. John wades in:

"Currently I am running my own communications business, and we have done several projects for your competitors. You may have noticed how well Clear Vision's stock has been doing lately. This is a result of the financial relations program I put together and implemented. I know I can do the same for your company. I've put my business up for sale and am looking for a position as a communications specialist. That is why I have called Mr. Fanter."

"This is about employment. Mr. Fanter will require a resume."

"I do not have a resume." (Allard speaks firmly, then shuts up.)

111

"Since this is about employment, you will have to submit a resume and go through Personnel."

"No, thanks, I've been that route before." (Again Allard shuts up.)

"Well, I don't believe I can help you."

"Fine. Please tell Mr. Fanter that I did call, since he may wonder why I didn't when he finds out later that I was available. I am sure that he will want to get in touch if you see fit to tell him why I called. Again, my name is Allard, A-L-L-A-R-D, and I am at 617-555-6345. Thank you for the help, Bruce . . . it is Bruce, isn't it?"

"Yes, Bruce Mapes."

Something like this might work. If it doesn't, relax and concentrate on another target. You might not be content working with that combination of boss and secretary anyway.

However, if the target still seems worthy of your persistence, try a dawn patrol or night mission. Call the Decision Maker before or after normal business hours when the saber tooth is not on guard duty. Your quarry may be in the office early, late, or both, and may be a compulsive phone answerer. Then you've got him. I used this technique and succeeded in reaching a senior vice president of North American Aviation who had promised to call back but never seemed to get around to it.

Your attitude in trying to get through to DMs must be that you have something to say, and if you are persistent enough you can succeed in talking to anyone, even the President of the United States. It may take some time to make the connection, but if your conversation is worthy of presidential attention you will get there in the end. This does not mean that you can convince a Decision Maker to hire you when you are not needed. Whether you choose to make a cold call or to write and follow up by phone, you can target an existing open position or create a requirement based on your background, but there is no way you can get yourself hired if there is no real need.

Decision Makers

DMs will frequently fail to return your call. Apply the Rule of Three. If you get no callback after you have left word three times, write the target off. Three times and you are persistent, four and you are a pest.

Another rebuff you will get from DMs is to be told the company is laying off. This means not merely "no," but "hell, no." Ask the Decision Maker if he or she knows of anyone who is hiring. If the company were hiring, would your background fit? Ask if you are on the right track. The DM will help.

You may be told there are no openings, which is only "no," not "hell, no." This leaves the door open for someone who really fits . . . someone who might be you. This is your chance to create a market for what you have to offer. You should have prepared a script to tell the DM what you will do to make him or her look good.

"Ms. Bright, I believe that by applying the new techniques I have developed you will be able to reduce your manufacturing costs through engineering change. My conservative estimate, based on what I know about your products and sales volume, is for an 8 percent improvement in six months. This will cover my salary and ten times that for the stockholders."

If Ms. Bright really is, she will meet with you.

If the DM tells you your background does not fit, either you have picked the wrong target or you have not gotten your point across. Give it another go with a presentation like the foregoing.

If the Decision Maker tries to put you off by asking you to send a resume, don't. Say something like this:

"Mr. Dillon, what else can I tell you? I have spent eight years running my own business, bringing it to annual sales of $750,000 from scratch. Prior to that, I spent seven years with Loomis Laboratories, where I was Director of Communications. Our annual reports were consistently rated among the top ten. I would like to meet with you so we can discuss my background."

Then, if the DM still insists on having a resume first, the ball is in your court. You must make a judgment call. Either forget the whole thing on the assumption that the request for a resume is nothing but a kiss-off, take the time to send your resume (you have nothing to lose), or, if it seems worth the effort, drop off the resume and try for an impromptu meeting.

You may be told that it is necessary to go through the personnel department. This is a kiss-off, too. Parry with a rephrasing of how you will make the DM look good and press again for an interview.

The worst treatment you may get from the DM is to be hung up on. There is no recourse in this case. Just be thankful you don't have to work for this person.

Leverage from the Top

There is one surefire way of getting a DM to listen to you. Suppose Ralph Miller has heard that there is an opening for a general manager in one of the divisions of a company, and he wants to get through to the Decision Maker. He researches the company and learns that the Group Vice President, his target's boss, is named Melvin Pringle. Ralph calls the switchboard, finds out the name of Mr. Pringle's secretary, and asks to be connected with her:

"Mary Quick, my name is Ralph Miller. I'm calling from Oregon."

"Yes, Mr. Miller. How can I help you?"

"I am a management specialist. I know your company has a division that is in need of a general manager. I asked to talk to you because I'm sure you can direct me to the person who would be most interested in my background."

At this point, Ms. Quick will attempt to shunt you off to the director of personnel.

"Mr. Miller, you should call Barry Bloom. He is Personnel Director for our Sunray Division. He will know of all the division's personnel requirements."

(If you cannot avoid this handoff, drop the whole thing. You will get nowhere with a personnel director. You'd be better off answering an ad for the general manager job when it appears or approaching another company or even mowing the lawn.)

"Ms. Quick, Mr. Bloom will not be able to appreciate what I can do for the division. My expertise can turn Sunray's business around. I'm sure the top man will want to know this."

"The President of the Sunray Division is Alex Riggor."

Ralph's next call is to Mr. Riggor. It goes like this:

"Hello, this is Mr. Riggor's office. Tess speaking. Can I help you?"

"Tess, this is Ralph Miller calling from Oregon. Is Mr. Riggor in?"

"He is in, but he is tied up in a meeting. Can I have him call you?"

"Please. My name is Ralph Miller, M-I-L-L-E-R. I'm calling at the suggestion of Mr. Pringle's office. It concerns general management."

Ralph has said the magic words, "Mr. Pringle's office." Riggor will call him back simply on the principle that any friend of Pringle's should be a friend of his. Ralph can be preparing to win an interview while waiting for the return call.

The procedure involved a number of people:

- Ralph Miller, job candidate
- The switchboard operator
- Mary Quick, secretary to Mr. Pringle
- Melvin Pringle, Group Vice President
- Barry Bloom, Personnel Director, Sunray Division
- Tess, secretary to Mr. Riggor
- Alex Riggor, President, Sunray Division

It took a lot of maneuvering and telephoning, but, as a result, Ralph has a clear shot at the Decision Maker he has targeted. Without the magic words, "Mr. Pringle's office," he might not have gotten so far.

Help!

You have been advised to ask the Decision Maker for help. Do this with everyone as a matter of course. "I need your help" is a magic phrase that works. You will be pleased with the reaction and the results. And, again, what do you have to lose?

Be Prepared

You always must be prepared before you initiate or return a call, just as if you were about to make a speech (because you *are* about to). Review in your mind:

- Whom you are calling.
- Your objective.
- The key points to be made.
- Your action step.

A particular case would look something like this:

- Person you are calling: Paul Hooper, Second Shift Manager, Bright Line Mills, Inc.
- Your objective: To get an in-person interview.
- The key points to be made (where you reiterate the contents of your letter):
  Your experience with a competitor.
  Your awards for production cost savings.
  Your invention of the speed bobbin.
- Your action step: To request an in-person interview.

This readiness is of fundamental importance. Remember the detailers, the people who sell to doctors. Because they are allowed very little time with the physician, they must make very efficient presentations, selling one product on the way in, one at the desk, and another on the way out. They are equipped with effective sales aids so they can accomplish this. Before they get to the doctor's office they are ready. Like them, you must be thoroughly prepared before you make that key phone call.

While I was at Forty-Plus, I sent out over 200 of those old-fashioned broadcast letters. When I finally got one telephone response, I became so excited that I rushed to the phone, completely unprepared. I blew the opportunity. I was like a detailer who arrived in the doctor's office without sales aids.

Let's look more closely at my own experience of unpreparedness. I had sent my letter to the president of a large aerospace company. He liked what he read and referred my paperwork to one of his group vice presidents, who was looking for a general manager. The VP called and left word at the Forty-Plus number that was my "executive office." So far so good.

I bolted. I should have gone through my files and refreshed my memory about the company and the man I had written to. Then I should have gone on to research the man who had called and the products in his group. Instead, I rushed to the quiet room and returned the call, completely unprepared. The guy ended up cutting me to pieces.

> "What? You are not a general manager now, but you used to be? You're out of work? What do you know about the product lines in my division? You're a chemical engineer . . . what makes you think you can do mechanical engineering work?"

I made no presentation. I had no answers. I was completely unprepared. In my excitement at finally getting a response after all those letters, I must have imagined that all I had to do to get hired was return the call. The phone interview ended abruptly:

> "You don't sound like you would be a very good general manager for any of my divisions. Goodbye."

Whether I would have been successful in getting an invitation for a personal interview if I had prepared properly for this phone encounter is still a question. Mr. VP came across as negative from the start, and I felt that he was probably resentful because his boss had told him to make the call. That is not the point. The lesson is that I was unprepared and did not take advantage of the opportunity I had struggled to earn.

If you plan your calls a day in advance using the techniques suggested next, not only will you have a checklist for the next day's work, but you will have had the time to prepare yourself psychologically for what is to come. I have learned that placing a few "practice calls" in the morning also helps me get up to speed. This might mean checking on the stationery order, canceling my appointment with the dentist, calling my broker, or making other everyday calls. This is a little like the fighter who shadowboxes around the ring before the first round. It loosens me up so I am more effective when it counts. Try it.

I have also learned that on certain days I should stay away from the phone altogether. These are days when my mind is full of boggles and my tongue is all thumbs. I now know enough to abandon Ma Bell on these days and do much-needed filing. If I must communicate, I use Uncle Sam's mail or the fax machine. And sometimes I just go fishing. Even if I catch no fish, I know I am ahead, because I haven't wasted opportunities by making ineffectual calls.

Planning for Inbound Calls

Planning for a call that you are going to make is relatively easy. Planning for those you are going to get is more difficult by far. You are well into your campaign. The tools are busy. All the pathways have been activated. Calls will arrive in response to the full range of your efforts: rifle-shot letters, answers to ads, the activities of headhunters, employment applications, the networking of friends and associates, and the calls you yourself have placed. You have to be alert, knowledgeable, responsive, and convincing in answering each call. Believe me, there is nothing more embarrassing or less impressive than fuzziness about which ad you answered, what letter you sent, or which call you placed. It is a disaster when you can't

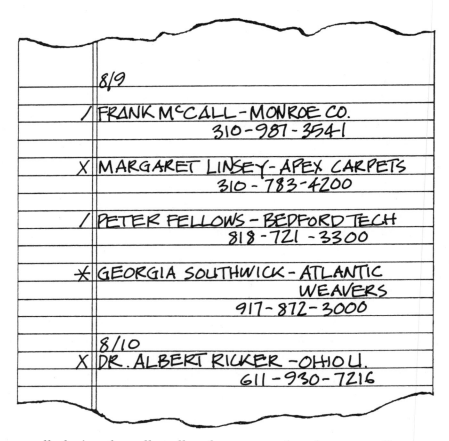

8/9

/ FRANK McCALL - MONROE CO.
310-987-3541

X MARGARET LINSEY - APEX CARPETS
310-783-4200

/ PETER FELLOWS - BEDFORD TECH
818-721-3300

✳ GEORGIA SOUTHWICK - ATLANTIC
WEAVERS
917-872-3000

8/10
X DR. ALBERT RICKER - OHIO U.
611-930-7216

recall placing the call at all and a catastrophe when you call someone a second time as if you had never called before.

In my recruiting work, I place at least twenty-five phone calls a
day. About a third of these will result in callbacks. My business
would be a shambles if I did not have a system that enabled me to
focus immediately on my plan for each call as it is returned. To
ensure this, as I place each call I record it in a small notebook. I
record the name of the person called, the company, and the phone
number. If the call is completed when placed, I put an "X" in the
first column. If I have left a message and expect a callback, I put a
"/" in the first column. (When the call is finally completed, so is the
"X.") A quick glance down the first column tells me which callbacks
are outstanding. The first column is blank if a call is still to be
placed. An asterisk indicates that the call was incomplete and can-
celled.

I have a file for each client, which I update with every call. I also
have a sheet for each of my candidates, which is updated after every

call, just as your medical records are updated after each visit to the doctor. Files and sheets corresponding to expected callbacks are kept at the ready on my desk. Several times a day I review all the outstanding callbacks, some of which can be several days old. These procedures prevent me from going blank—at least most of the time—when a voice says, for instance, "This is Wendell Willard returning your call." My emergency procedure when I don't remember Wendell is to hang up. Later, when mental gymnastics have finally enabled me to identify him, I call back and apologize for the interruption, blaming it on the phone company. (I am one of its big customers and feel it owes me this.) This is a useful procedure, and if you are really working the new-job problem, you will be happy to include the technique in your repertoire.

In job hunting, being prepared for all possible callbacks is even more complex than it is in recruiting. As stated before, you may receive calls in response to your own phone calls, as well as to the letters and ad answers you have sent out, at any time. You must have at the ready your notes on the calls you have placed, plus your files of letters sent and advertisements answered. These must be reviewed regularly if you're going to have half a chance of being responsive each time your phone rings. If you are going to be able to "act like you've been there before" on the phone, you will have to employ good clerical procedures.

Act Like You've Been There Before

In discussing rejection, I mentioned the cumulonimbus clouds encountered by pilots flying across Florida on summer afternoons. One summer's day I made such a flight across the state. My copilot had just been reactivated to flight status as a result of the Korean fracas. He had been flying nothing but a desk for the last five years and suddenly found himself strapped to an airplane that was being battered by a line of thunderstorms and was struggling to hold itself together. Fear gripped him to such an extent that he began to hyperventilate. This definitely was not the way for him to dust off his wings. I had been flying regularly and knew there was no real danger. I stayed calm. He could not. A couple of local flights would have enabled him to get back into the swing of things.

You now know the important elements of telephone style. With them, you will have no need to come across like Caspar Milquetoast or a reluctant door-to-door salesman. Apply these techniques to every call you make. Practice on your insurance agent, banker, lawyer, bookie, etc. Make one or two warm-up calls. Then, acting like you've been there before, reach out and grab that DM!

Chapter 10

The Personnel Department

"It is possible to get a better job in spite of the personnel department."

There is no way you are going to get on the payroll without becoming involved with the people in the personnel department. If you're lucky, the contact will be limited to signing the forms that will get you on the payroll. Unfortunately, it is likely to be much more. Take heart. It is possible to get a better job in spite of the personnel department.

Overcommitment

The head of personnel can have any of several titles, depending on the school of management attended or the philosophy of management adopted by those in charge:

Vice President		Human Resources
Director	of	Employee Relations
Manager		Industrial Relations
Supervisor		Personnel

Whatever the title, the position entails all of the following responsibilities and more:

Community/public relations
Organizational development
Recruiting
   Management
   Professional
   College
   Nonexempt (unsalaried)

Employment research (demographics, test evaluations, etc.)
Training
Management development
Manpower planning
Executive compensation
Employee benefits
Equal opportunity administration
Labor relations
  Contract negotiation
  Grievances
  Elections
Safety
Environmental protection
Personnel records

Personnel departments obviously have more than enough to do, which reminds me of what happened to the Lenkal Naval Base. The Mantooks feared invasion from their neighbors, the Ruffers. It was decided to establish a naval base to oversee the Mantooka Straits and report on Ruffer naval activity. The outpost was soon attacked, not by the Ruffers but by progress. First an officers' club was built. A club for the enlisted men and a commissary soon followed, and a motor pool became necessary to provide transportation between the two. Then came the post theater and the dispensary. The Lenkal Naval Base soon became important enough to be commanded by Rear Admiral "Riverboat" Stripes. A month after he took over, the commander received a sharp wire from headquarters demanding to know why the regular report on Ruffer naval activity had not been submitted. Admiral Stripes responded, "I've got a naval base to run and can't be bothered counting ships."

The personnel department is established because a growing organization needs to hire people. But it becomes so involved with its peripheral duties and with the people already hired that its original mission is neglected. I have never, never worked with any personnel officer whose time was not seriously overcommitted.

Slow Progress

If you are pursuing a new job through the personnel department, this overcommitment means slow progress toward a meeting with a Decision Maker. Caught in the confusion of shared responsibility and paperwork that exists between the personnel department and the person with the vacancy, you are on a muddy track. One party is always waiting for the other to act: the DM awaits more candidates and the personnel department is waiting for comments on the candidates it has already submitted (while distracted by its other duties). Meanwhile customers may be suffering, because while the slot remains open, work remains undone.

If top management dictates that all hiring contacts must go through the personnel department, the mud becomes quicksand. My search firm was once asked to fill a manufacturing position for a large company in Cleveland. When I attempted to talk to the Decision Maker, I was told, "All contacts must be made through the Vice President of Human Relations," and I was not provided with important details about the position to be filled. It became apparent that the Human Relations bottleneck would add weeks to the search, and I would be trying to fill a position for which the specifications were interpreted by a personnel officer and most likely did not match the requirements of the DM. To zero in on the target would take a very time-consuming process of trial and error. Just to complicate things, my sources in the company reported that the Vice President of Human Relations was the President's brother-in-law and was ready to pull rank at the least hint that someone was trespassing on his territory. I left this search for some other recruiter.

Other Limitations

In addition to overcommitment, there are other pressures that affect the personnel department's recruiting efficiency. One is a fear of employing the wrong person and losing a reputation for finding only the best. Some departments may feel that it is better not to fill a job rather than take a chance on hiring a misfit. Playing it safe is easy to do when you are not directly responsible for the work to be done. (The manager with a schedule to meet obviously has a very different bias: after the vacancy exists for some time, it's "Let's try someone!")

Money can be a factor. Candidates' travel and living expenses, relocation costs, etc., often come out of the personnel budget. One way to stay within budget is not to hire. If the work does not get done, that is not personnel's concern.

The fact that the people in personnel are not in the mainstream of the business can make them somewhat touchy. For example, when shipments are running late, the personnel department is not called to join in the recovery plan. Since its function is not tactically critical, personnel becomes a great place for companies to park the people they don't know what else to do with. Personnel is not the most prestigious place to work, and this can have subtle effects on its ability, or willingness, to help you.

I had been given a search for a technical service representative. This was a particularly difficult assignment because of the combination of talents required: technical knowledge of the product plus customer skills. After several weeks, I recruited an ideal candidate. The personnel director of the company in question insisted on a telephone screening, which went badly. The candidate was turned off. I was able to convince him to agree to an in-person interview, but the director of personnel insisted on screening the candidate personally before involving the Decision Maker. The personnel director was, in fact, trying to act like the Decision Maker. He acted as if he knew the intricacies of the job and tried to suggest that his decision, if not final, was at least critical. He did not sell the company, the position, or the career path. My candidate ended up walking away, completely frustrated by a meeting that was a waste of his time. I was confident that, had the Decision Maker met this candidate, a marriage would have been made. The personnel director's ego got in the way of a good match.

The sum of all this is that those in personnel are overcommitted, overprotective, budget conscious, yet out of the mainstream. This means that the work of hiring, when handled by them, is often seriously slowed or stopped, and you should avoid going through them if at all possible.

When You Can't Avoid It

When you can't avoid the personnel department, remember to treat everyone in the organization as a mini–Decision Maker. A mini–DM is anyone between you and the DM who makes the final decision. Mini–DMs don't have the authority to award the job to you, but they do have enough clout to see that you are eliminated. Remember the Decision Maker's code and convince all the people you meet with that, if they recommend you, you will make them look good. Remember the Miss America process, and keep your flaws to yourself. Remember the words of Johnny Mercer and "Accent-tchu-ate The Positive, E-lim-my-nate the negative. . . ."

Your initial contact with the personnel department will probably be a telephone interview. Telephone inquisitions are always crucial and deserve the separate chapter that follows. When the telephone interview is conducted by someone in the personnel department, special care must be taken. Just keep in mind that it is the personnel department's responsibility to reduce a large number of candidates to the few that get to the DM. It tends to be overprotective, preferring to find a flaw and cull rather than take a chance on hiring someone who may turn out to be less than perfect for the job, even if this means that the job may not be filled for a long time.

Not a Personnel Vendetta

This is not a campaign to discredit personnel departments. Neither is it a campaign to try and remedy their problems. I would not send you off into the Amazon without a map, and these remarks about personnel departments are only to educate you about what to expect in the real world of job search.

Of course, there are exceptions that emerge from the jungle. For several years I have worked with a Personnel Manager who is all the things a job candidate could hope for: knowledgeable, responsive, helpful, cooperative, and involved. He is in an organization that is growing rapidly and in need of highly skilled people. He understands that new employees are needed to get the products out the door on time and at a profit. He accepts the responsibility of doing all he can to fill critical positions. He is not concerned with protecting his ego or his empire. He is always aware of problems that need to be solved in the plant and is always there to help. Actually, he has recently overdone it, from my point of view. He has been promoted and is now Manager of Statistical Quality Assurance. I will miss him.

Another winner I've worked with is Personnel Manager for one of the divisions of a large corporation. She is overworked like all of them, eating a sandwich at her desk and returning calls after hours. She is *involved* with the fortunes of her division's operations. She's there helping to get the product out the door on time and at a profit. Her time is spent building the organization, not protecting her own bailiwick. She won't last long. She will be promoted, and I will miss her, too.

In Conclusion

For you seekers of better jobs, here are some general conclusions about the people in personnel departments:

- They are usually overcommitted. They have too much to do to be able to do any one thing to the best of their ability.
- They tend to be overly cautious in hiring people, preferring to let a vacancy exist rather than take a chance on hiring a misfit.
- They may be working under budgetary pressures that slow the hiring process.
- They may have an exaggerated desire for the recognition of their importance to the company.

- They may be overly protective of their prerogatives in the organization.

Knowing these things, you are advised to avoid being caught in the web. Work directly with the Decision Maker whenever possible. Certainly never initiate contact with the personnel department. Research, inquire, and probe to identify the target Decision Maker. Failing to succeed at that, contact the president or department head. Don't direct your ad responses to the named person unless you are sure this is the DM. If a blind ad gives sufficient clues, do your Sherlock Holmes impersonation to identify the company and Decision Maker. But don't waste your skills as a private eye only to discover the director of personnel.

Once the line of communication has been established, continue to work directly with the DM. Sneak around the people in personnel if necessary. The Decision Maker wants them out of the way as much as you do. Of course, he or she must avoid stepping on toes but will cooperate with you if you are discreet.

If you have just walked in or are applying for a position at entry level, you are going to have to go through the personnel office. Don't fight it. Make everyone in the personnel department feel important. Any one of them can leave your paperwork rotting in an in-basket. Make an effort to convince the sundry mini–Decision Makers you meet that they will look good by boosting you on your way to the DM. And finally, be particularly careful not to let negatives or flaws appear in your communications with the personnel office. Remember, their line of least resistance is to cull.

The degree to which you are likely to become involved with the people in personnel depends on how high up the career ladder you are aiming. When Lee Iacocca moved from Ford to Chrysler, I imagine that personnel was like a guardian angel . . . invisible, while taking care of the business of getting him on the payroll. On the other hand, the person who applies for the machinist's job advertised on the company marquee will be in the hands of the personnel office and may not meet the supervisor until the first day of work. People hired directly from college campuses are sometimes in the same situation. If this is you, don't fight it. There is no way out. Apply what you learn here to make your encounters with the personnel department as effective as possible.

Chapter 11

The Telephone Interview

"You have won the first round when the telephone interview ends with an invitation to meet in person."

It would be great if you could avoid telephone interviews entirely, but you can't do it. On the road to your new job, you will probably be interviewed one or more times by phone. The occasions can range from simple fact-finding calls preceding the invitation to meet to in-depth interrogations designed to determine whether an invitation should be made at all. Think of the latter as being like the elimination rounds in tennis, golf, or drag racing. It's a game you have to play but can't win outright. All you can hope to do is keep from losing.

Telephone interviews are tricky. It is very easy to be scratched from the competition if the call goes badly. At this stage, the caller's task is usually to reduce a list of candidates to two or three finalists. Remember the Miss America process and the resulting necessity for you to avoid flaws and negatives. This is more difficult to do over the phone. Your voice must carry the show. You don't have the benefit of your appearance, posture, or presence. Charisma will not work for you. There is no eye contact or body language to read. It is hard to get a feel for a person through the receiver. Your best tactic is to reach your objective as quickly as possible and get offstage. That objective, the only objective of any telephone interview, is *to win an in-person interview.* This is not the time to try to win the job.

If you are unavoidably caught in the clutches of the personnel department or have to relate to mini–Decision Makers, your goal is to get them to boost you to a meeting with the Decision Maker. If you have the DM on the line, press for the meeting directly. Don't provide any unnecessary information or ask any needless questions. Remember the arguments for keeping your resume to one page. The same applies here. Irrelevant information increases the chances of showing flaws that can lead to your being culled. Keep it simple.

Who's Calling?

Calls can come from any or all of three directions: the personnel department, mini–Decision Makers, and the Decision Maker. Be sure to identify the person calling. Ask for name *and* title. You must be absolutely clear about who is on the other end of the line. Don't get caught thinking you are talking to the personnel department when it is really the Decision Maker or vice versa. Your approach will be different in each case. You are going to want to convince the people from personnel that the way for them to look good is to pass you on up to the DM. You are going to want to impress the DM with how great he or she will look once you're on the staff.

Personnel

A phone interview with someone from the personnel department is perilous. Of all the people who may question you by phone, the caller from personnel will have the longest list of candidates to cull. He or she will also be pressured by the factors discussed in the previous chapter, principally overcommitment and a strong desire to play it safe. The result is that there will be an extraordinary degree of sensitivity to negatives and flaws. You must be equally sensitive to avoid giving any negative impressions.

Mini–Decision Makers

Remember that mini–Decision Makers are intermediaries between you and the Decision Maker. They have been chosen to do the legwork for the final authority on the assumption that they know more about the position than the personnel department does (a valid assumption). Generally speaking, mini–DMs are not a serious hurdle unless you come on as a threat to their jobs. They will probably not question you about your salary requirements but will be more likely to concentrate on product-line experience and similar details.

Decision Makers

Any conversation with a Decision Maker is crucial. Without his or her blessing at every stage, six strong men will carry your candidacy out by the handles. With DMs, the cautions about negatives and flaws apply in spades . . . and they apply even more so on the telephone.

The DM's approach can cover the spectrum from your alma mater to sales techniques to past accomplishments, either yours or the DM's. Decision makers have free rein. It's their ball, and you can expect to encounter every sort of innovation in interview technique.

Be Ready

Be sure you have reliable, professional telephone service. That is perhaps the biggest advantage of being provided with outplacement. If you and your spouse are the only ones who are going to be answering when the phone beckons, that might work, but if you have teenagers at home, get yourself a phone that is dedicated solely to your job hunt. Make sure you have a dependable answering service, whether live or electronic. As recently as five years ago, answering machines were frowned on by many people, particularly people in business, but today it is impossible to avoid these devices. Their invasion has been successful because they speed the wheels of commerce. If you feel you cannot afford a separate phone and answering machine, just relax and take the next job that comes along.

Review the chapter on telephone style. Install administrative procedures that will enable you to be sharp when a telephone interview happens. Have your telephone log, ad answers, and letters by the telephone, not in your briefcase and not under the desk. Make sure you review these materials often to prime your memory. Be ready.

Remember the pitiful way I handled the *only* telephone interview I had as a result of my 200-letter campaign at Forty-Plus. I was completely unprepared when I returned the call. When you have the advantage of calling back, make the most of it. Plan your call to zero in on the particular opportunity. Anticipate the questions you may be asked.

You should have a general script written out. (No, you are not going to recite it from memory like the Lord's Prayer, but you will have thought out your overall approach and have it in mind.) On top of this general script, fit in the specific points that will make the Decision Maker look good in each case. Don't expect every call to go exactly as you planned, but if you have prepared, you are bound to be ahead of the game, and maybe even in charge some of the time.

Control the Timing

When you have the advantage of being the one to call back, you can pick the time you call and the place you call from. If you are at home, make sure the kids are out of range and the TV is not blaring. You want to be able to concentrate on the call. If you are at the office, never call when there is a possibility of your boss walking in or a coworker picking up the extension. Control the calling environment so you will be relaxed and sharp. You have invested time, dollars, and vitality in getting this opportunity. Don't blow it.

If a call catches you at a bad time, say so.

"I have an office full of people. Can I call you back?"

"You have caught me at a bad time. Houseguests are about to leave. Can I call you back?"

And if you draw a blank when you hear the caller's name and company, get the phone number and arrange to call back later (after the fog lifts).

Make Appointments

In my recruiting work, I strive to avoid having my candidates interviewed by phone, particularly when there is no cross-country travel involved. I press for the first contact to be in person. When phone conversations can't be avoided, I make definite appointments. I tell the client to place the call at a specific time and to enter it on his or her calendar like any other appointment. I instruct the candidate to be ready at the designated phone.

You must establish the same discipline. When you are told that you will be called, immediately establish a date, time, and place. Make the point that you are treating the telephone appointment just as you would an office visit, and you expect the calling party to do the same. However, don't be overly optimistic that all your phone encounters will take place as scheduled. Frankly, DMs do not give them the same importance as meetings in the office, and even those don't always take place on time. But make the effort, and you will come out ahead. You will get a commitment from the Decision Maker, and the effort made to meet this commitment will be a good measure of the DM's interest.

Recently I set a telephone date for Margot: the DM was to call her at home at 6:30 p.m. When I followed up later that evening I found that the call had never come through. The next morning the DM excused himself by saying he had been caught in traffic with no phone in the car. The call was then rescheduled for 5:30 that afternoon. It came through at about 7:30. It was clear to Margot that the client was not very interested. I agreed. She was placed with another company.

If you make a telephone appointment, you can be as ready as it's possible to be. The call will be treated as more significant by both you and the DM. And, if you're lucky, it just might come off on schedule.

Anticipate

Think how the call is likely to develop. What will be important to the person at the other end of the receiver? What are his or her key "look-goods"? What are the strengths of your candidacy? The weaknesses? Construct an outline for the call, including:

- Examples of how you have made your bosses look good.
- Accomplishments that relate directly to the job at hand.
- Accomplishments in areas in which you are weak.
- Answers to the main questions you expect to be asked.
- A ready answer to the question, "Why do you want to change jobs?"
- A ready answer to the question, "Why do you want to work for this company?"
- A ready answer to the question, "How much money do you want?"

You must exercise absolute discipline in your response to this last question.

NEVER, NEVER, NEVER ANSWER THE QUESTION OF
HOW MUCH MONEY YOU WANT.

Chapters 14 and 17 cover the negotiation of compensation. Here I would only like to warn you that you are very likely to be asked about money over the phone, particularly by the personnel department, whose main interest is to cull. One of the easiest ways for them to narrow the field is to eliminate the candidates who seem to be asking for too much money. More on this important point later.

Follow the Interviewer's Lead

The interviewer will clue you in on the correct responses if you just listen. Be alert for such statements as "I do not see any experience managing industrial properties in your background." This remark is made to see if you will confirm the impression. It is your cue to fill in what is suspected to be a blank. This is no time to break out in a rash of humility. If you have managed even one industrial building, tout your experience.

Suppose I were being interviewed for a job as a pilot and was asked if I had experience with gliders. The true answer could be either "not much" or "yes." Even though my experience amounted to only one glider landing, my answer would be "yes."

During any interview, particularly one conducted on the phone, reach deep into the reservoir of your experience and tout yourself, as long as you don't try to parlay your experience repairing watches into brain surgery or the like. You are in this tournament to win a job in which you are going to make the Decision Maker look good better than anyone else can. Don't let a fit of modesty on your part deprive the DM of what DMs want most.

Parry Questions

Parrying questions must be part of your telephone technique. Realizing that you cannot use all your firepower over the phone, you will want to divert key questions and answers to the in-person interview. This is an important tactic for getting you to a better field on which to play; in other words, a great way to press for a meeting.

> **"Mr. Manahan, that is an important question, and I have four years of applicable experience. I cannot cover this adequately over the phone. I suggest that we discuss it in person."**

This parries the question, whets the DM's appetite, and presses for a meeting. You can use this tactic twice, maybe even three times, per telephone interview. As you constructed your outline in preparation for the call, you identified important questions that might be asked. These are the ones you can suggest would be answered best in person (when you will have all your interview prowess working for you).

Be a "Closer"

Here is some sales jargon: at this point, you want to make an "assumptive close" with a "choice question." In other words, you should conduct your telephone interview as if there is no question of your being given an in-person interview. The Decision Maker simply has a choice as to when it will take place.

131

> **"Ms. Delaney, I am very much interested in the position we have talked about. I want the opportunity to meet with you and to answer your important questions in person. I don't feel I can do justice to my background in gourmet restaurant management over the phone. I can be in your office Wednesday morning, or would Thursday afternoon be better?"**

Not subtle, but that's not what you're trying to be. You are after a job offer, and the in-person interview is the apogee of your effort.

Lynn Longmyer's Telephone Interview

We left Lynn Longmyer with the first version of her resume, the one aimed at customer service in an ad agency. Six weeks have passed. Since Lynn is not a very good typist, she has found a public stenographer who has word processing capability. Her basic resume resides at the ready in the word processor. It can be pinpointed in a matter of minutes to fit any target. Lynn has had a second phone and an answering machine installed at home. Her friends have been alerted in writing, as have her business and social associates. So far she has answered fifteen selected advertisements, each carefully "word matched." Her letter campaign has involved nineteen rifle shots, each one tuned to a particular company. She is in the process of selecting further ads and targeted companies and is now contemplating sending her resume to recruiters.

The phone rings and Lynn answers it:

> "Lynn Longmyer speaking."

> **"Hello, this is Al Bennet. You answered our ad in the *Atlanta Tribune.*"**

> "Hello, Mr. Bennet. What company are you with?"

> **"I'm with Bryant & Matson Advertising."**

> "I know your company but do not remember contacting you. Was it a blind ad?"

> **"Yes, you wrote to Box AC109. We advertised for someone in sales administration."**

> "Yes, I have my copy here. Mr. Bennet, what is your title?"

"I'm the Promotional Director."

"Will this position report to you?"

"Yes. Your background seems to fit our requirements, and I called to learn more about you."

"Fine. What can I tell you that is not on the resume?"

"The product lines you have worked with are somewhat different from those of our clients. We deal mostly with consumer goods of the sort found in supermarkets. You don't seem to have related experience."

"Mr. Bennet, I did not mention it in my resume, but my prize-winning logo design was for the Babcock Bread people. You may recall having seen it. I also did graphics and wrote copy for their cookies and cakes. This experience has given me a good understanding of the needs of clients in that market."

"That sounds good. You did not indicate your salary level. How much money do you want?"

"At this stage, I am looking for a career opportunity. That is what is important to me. I believe the money will follow, because I have faith in what I can do. I proved my ability at Eric Hamilton & Associates. In addition to the $250,000 client I mentioned in my resume, there were other contracts I won for the company. The work I brought in enabled my boss to move up a notch, and he took me with him."

"What has your income been while free-lancing?"

"It has varied. Hills and valleys. But I have not been working full-time. If I had, I would have been making about $50,000 a year."

"Why do you want to go back to full-time employment?"

"It has always been my plan that after the family was started I would resume my career."

"Lynn, will the children be a distraction? What will you do when one of them is sick? What about school vacations?"

"Mr. Bennet, that is not a problem. It is understandably something you would like to explore in detail. The phone is no place for that, so I would like to meet with you. I can be in your office at 10 on Wednesday morning, or would Thursday morning be better?"

"OK, Ms. Longmyer, let's make it Thursday at 10."

"Thank you, Mr. Bennet. I will be there."

It would be great if all calls went as smoothly as this. There is a reasonable chance they will if you anticipate questions and are ready with the answers.

Lynn's example can be used to make some important points. First, Lynn had her correspondence files at the ready, and as soon as she identified the company and advertisement in question, she was able to pull out the appropriate letter. She identified the caller as the Promotional Director and definitely the Decision Maker. She responded positively to his negative question about her product experience. She handled the salary query not by stating her desired salary but by giving some idea of her level. Her response to the question concerning her decision to return to work was matter-of-fact and professional. She parried the one about the children, suggesting that the details could not be handled adequately over the phone. This set the scene for her to ask the "choice question" and arrange the in-person interview.

My favorite high school teacher often reminded us that "the end is the test." Lynn Longmyer earned the chance to be one of those tested, and to be among those tested is the apogee of your job-search efforts. You have won the first round when the telephone interview ends with an invitation to meet in person. Now on to the next chapter!

Chapter 12

Preparing for the In-Person Interview

"Skillful use of the tools and pathways has earned you an in-person interview. The prize is won when you get the job offer."

Approach your in-person interview with the knowledge that the process of winning a job offer is a delicate one. Let one flaw show or one negative slip through and you could be eliminated from the race. In your job search, skillful use of the tools and pathways has earned you an in-person interview. The prize is won when you get the job offer. So you want to eliminate those negatives, if anything erring on the side of overcompensation.

Be Even Readier

Everything that has been said about preparing for a telephone interview applies here, except more so. When I am preparing to present a candidate to a new client, I must first learn all I can about the company and the Decision Maker. I review the company's product literature and financial reports. I talk to their sales department. I search for someone who has worked there and has recently left, since this is often the best source of information about the company and the DM (allowing for possible sour grapes). You should know your target in similar detail.

Before deciding how much energy you want to put into preparation for the in-person interview, consider the value of the time you will have eyeball-to-eyeball with the DM. Consider your efforts to get this far: the letters, ad answers, resume revisions, phone calls, company research, word processing, etc. Figure the dollars you have spent on postage, telephone use (including your separate line and answering service or machine), secretarial time, stationery, and gasoline. Calculate the hours all this has taken and put a price on them.

A hypothetical candidate is out of work and has conducted a three-month search that results in four interviews, each lasting an hour and a half. The candidate has done everything that could be done to win these interviews. Let's put a price of $5 per hour on time spent and assume a 40-hour week.

40 hours per week at $5 per hour for 12 weeks	$2400
Phone installation	50
Monthly phone bill (including answering service)	150
Personalized stationery	100
Postage	200
Secretarial and word processing services	600
Gasoline, lunches, parking, etc.	200
TOTAL	$3700

For all this, the candidate earns 6 hours with Decision Makers at a cost of roughly $600 per hour. (This price is conservative, since our job seeker was willing to work for $5 an hour. Are you?) This candidate was out of work, so the cost of each in-person interview must be increased to reflect living costs during the search period. Calculate your own price for an audience with a DM. You will see that you have made a substantial investment and that the effort to prepare for the interview is well spent to protect this investment.

Of course, if money's not a problem, you can skip all this math. And if you're not out of work, your efforts can be more casual, but in the long run, the price of an in-person interview will not be cheap.

Still More Anticipation

Your intensive fact-finding has equipped you to judge the issues that will be of greatest interest to the DM and to predict the areas that he or she will want to explore. If you are an engineer and you have learned that the company interviewing you needs new products, you can expect to be asked about your new-product ideas. If you are an accountant and have found that the company's profitability is low, you want to stress your skill in applying cost-control techniques. Manufacturing people should emphasize their ability to cut scrap. Administrators should describe the way they speeded work flow and improved profit.

All it takes is about 10 minutes' thought to plan how and when to strike the right chords. The day before the interview, or at least a couple of hours before, set aside 10 minutes for this planning. Ten minutes may not sound like much, but it's really all you need to set yourself apart in the right way from the candidates who are in there winging it.

Prior to any in-person interview, you should go back to the "opportunity questions" in Chapter 7. Though most people consider them stressful, in our book they are chances to be positive. Pay particular attention to "Why did you leave your job?" Just as surely as you have to pay taxes, you are going to have to respond to this one, perhaps several times. Your ability to explain this in a positive way for any job you have held should be so well rehearsed it is practically a reflex. There is no excuse for you to strike out on this one. You know the DM is going to throw this fastball, so be ready to hit a dinger.

You no longer have to be prepared to parry questions as you did for the telephone interview. The sparring is over, and you are now playing for keeps.

Types of Interviewers

You will have chances to try your poise on several different types of interviewer. In fact, I suspect there are as many different types as there are people, but they can be classified in three broad groups: the self-made expert, the inexperienced interviewer, and the professional manager.

The Self-Made Expert

This type of interviewer is gruff at first (but can mellow), presses for answers, gives a demonstration of being in charge, appears defensive, and most likely is. She or he will have many preconceptions about the position and the perfect candidate to fill it. Your task with these people will be to discover the precise nature of their preconceptions through careful consideration of the questions you are asked. Then, if you decide it's a job you can do and would like to do, you can adapt your prepared "look-good" material accordingly. This type of interviewer will be especially interested in looking good.

Let me tell you about my "fireplug episode." I was interviewing for a sales position with the Vice President of Marketing of a computer company. He and I were getting along just great. He had taken off his coat and rolled up his sleeves, and was using flip charts to explain the details of the position, which he felt was just right for me. I was slouched comfortably in my chair with my legs stretched out, hardly an eager-beaver posture but suited to the informal tenor of our discussion. Suddenly the door sprang open, and a little guy built like a fireplug peered in, said, "Let me know when you're through," and left. The Vice President and I continued our talk. I had the job. All that remained was for me to meet his boss.

You guessed it. The fireplug was the boss. He looked like the kind of guy who would jump out of his truck at a red light and beat on your hood just for the fun of it, and to make matters worse, I found out later that he had hurt his back and was in pain. I never did learn what he considered the qualifications for the job to be, though I did learn that slouching during an interview was not among them. I had flunked the instant he saw me draped in the chair, and now he had me sitting on its last 3 inches while he fired questions at me:

"What is the most important aspect of selling computers?"

"What is your technique for working with customers?"

"What is the first thing you would do on the job?"

"What makes our product the best?"

Before I could finish an answer, he shouted, "No, that's not it!" and fired the next one. There went the job. I thought of a great comeback for this treatment; the trouble is, I'm one of those people who always thinks of great comebacks *after* the moment has passed. I should have walked out. You should include this in your repertoire of useful tactics, along with hanging up the phone. Do not hesitate to walk out when a negative outcome is obvious.

In another instance, I was being interviewed for the position of Vice President of Marketing for a major industrial and aerospace instrumentation company. The President had come up through the engineering ranks and believed that the only way to sell was to engineer the product right in the first place so it would sell itself. Our debate was vigorous and at times heated. It lasted long after it became clear that our differences were insurmountable. In this case, I did cut the meeting short, but it should have been done sooner, when it first became obvious that I was not a viable candidate. When this happens to you, get offstage. Don't hang around.

The Inexperienced Interviewer

This type of interviewer is usually friendly, uncertain about what to cover, vague in response to your questions, and generally unsure of himself or herself. (How do I know? Only because I have been one.) With this person, you have a great opportunity to apply the knowledge and skills you have gained to direct the meeting toward

DM "look-goods" that will earn you the job offer. Don't take this type of interviewer lightly. Make the most of the chance.

The Professional Manager

This person will approach the interview as he or she does any meeting . . . fully prepared. When Robert McNamara was Secretary of Defense, the word in the Pentagon was that you had better have done your homework before a meeting with him. He was always the best prepared of anyone at the table. The professional manager approaches interviews in the same way.

As a DM, the professional manager will have a clear understanding of what is needed in the position, will have well-thought-out questions, will control the meeting, and generally will be less communicative than the other types. And the professional will also be the easiest to work with, because you have done your homework! You know the important aspects of the job. You can anticipate the questions and analyze them for the DM's emphasis. You can add your analysis of eye contact and your reading of body language to what you already know to zero in further on the important aspects of the position as the DM sees them.

Questions and Comments

At this stage, only two people's questions and comments matter: the Decision Maker's and yours. Forget the personnel department and the mini–DMs. The real Decision Maker's words are the ones you're interested in now, and because they show his or her hand, you can play yours to win the offer. Listen carefully, analyze, and promote yourself accordingly.

The Decision Maker's questions or comments will go something like this:

"You do not have much experience in selling fine jewelry."

"Have you ever audited a retail chain?"

"How about experience in computer-aided design?"

"Have you ever been involved in the manufacture of office furniture?"

"I see you are with a fast-food chain. Have you ever managed a gourmet restaurant?"

"I don't see anything here about investor relations."

"In our business, it is especially important to keep the bankers happy."

"We have a very difficult quality problem."

Think and respond carefully. The DM has announced his or her concerns about the position, about your candidacy, or about both. From these you know what the important "look-goods" are. Now go to your repertoire of skills and tout yourself. This will be easy because of the work you have done in anticipation of this moment. Don't give in to twinges of modesty or humility. Tout yourself. Remember my answer to the glider pilot question.

A Copy of Your Resume?

If you have been clever enough to get to the in-person interview without giving the Decision Maker a copy of your resume, that's great. The resume can plant unsuspected negatives and flaws in the mind of a DM, so why take the risk if you don't have to? However, now that you are face to face, you are going to be asked for a copy. Try to get away with a promise of leaving one at the end of the meeting. This way you can avoid a nitpicking analysis of what is printed and spend the valuable time together linking your background to the DM's need to look good. Never, never, never open an interview with "Here is a copy of my resume."

Your Questions

Prepare your questions ahead of time and ask them with care. There is one question that you *must* ask early in the meeting. Write it on a 3 × 5 card and put it in your purse or shirt pocket. (No, you aren't going to pull it out and recite from it. It's there as a reminder.)

> "Your personnel people and assistants have done a fine job of detailing the work to be done. However, it would be very helpful if you would describe it also. What do you consider to be the most important responsibilities of the job?"

Knowing what your interviewer considers to be important is the only way you can get a sight on the true bull's-eye. Otherwise it could be like shooting at ducks when you have to hit rabbits in order to win your date the stuffed poodle.

Feel free to ask about aspects of the job that have not been made explicit. You may have to hit on particular points to be a winner, and clear understanding of the situation is necessary to know which ones. But be careful in asking about the company. If you really want to know about sales, number of employees, major customers, most important products, etc., you can find these things out during the preparatory stages. Stay away from subjects that could be touchy, such as profits, union relations, or the news that the company just lost a large contract. You should have done your homework, you should know what you want to know, and you should ask just enough about company matters to seem genuinely interested.

Two years ago, I sponsored a classic confrontation between a client in Seattle and a candidate from Salt Lake City. The client came from a financial background, ran the business from the operating statement, and thrived on detail. The candidate was being interviewed for a market research position and was ideally suited for it by his education, experience, interest, and passion for detail. It appeared to be a great matchup.

I wish I had been a fly on the wall when these two met. From what I heard, the interview was the equivalent of an hour-long volley in tennis. The DM would ask a question only to have the candidate return one that triggered another from the DM, and so it went. The postinterview comment from both participants was "I could never work with anyone who wants that much detail." The candidate lost out on any chance of getting the job offer, and the client lost the chance of hiring a well-qualified person. I guess I lost, too. I never did place the interviewee and have not worked for the Seattle company since.

Ask all the questions necessary to your understanding of the job, ask enough about the company to show your interest, and then *listen*. You will get your turn as inquisitor *after you have the job offer*.

Needs, Benefits, and Features

Remember the "assumptive close" and the "choice question"? Well, here comes some more sales talk. "Needs," "benefits," and "features" are the bedrock of selling. You sales types who know all there is to know can skim over this section and sit back smugly working on your tans (or better still, working on revising your resume for the next target). The rest of us salespeople will be busy catching up.

Yes, we are all salespeople when it comes to the new-job search. You may not have thought of it in this light before, but you are going to be selling until your job campaign is over . . . selling *yourself.* Don't run right out and buy suede shoes or enroll in a Dale Carnegie course. All you need is right here, even if you've never sold anything in your life and feel you couldn't sell umbrellas in a monsoon.

The relationship between needs, benefits, and features is as follows: the salesperson sells the product's benefits that result from its features to satisfy customers' needs.

YOU SELL THE BENEFITS OF THE PRODUCT THAT
RESULT FROM ITS FEATURES TO SATISFY NEEDS.

Why all the fuss? Because this is what you will do to get the job offer. The Decision Maker's *need* is to look good. You are the product. Your *features* are the abilities that produced accomplishments that made your previous DMs look good. The *benefit* to the DM in hiring you is *looking good.*

Identify the Need

One of the quicksands neophyte salespeople sink into is trying to sell a product for which there is no need. Thomas Edison invented a system that would record the votes in Congress electrically. It never sold. There was no real need. Senators didn't want to vote by pushing a button. They wanted to give speeches. They wanted to lie in the weeds and see how the show of hands went before showing theirs.

Another man invented an egg-candling machine. It never sold. Farmers realized they could candle eggs with it for the rest of their lives and never save enough time to pay for the device. There was no real need.

The first step in selling is to identify the need. Fortunately, the hiring process is driven by a very basic need, the Decision Maker's need to look good. The nice thing about interviewing is that, one way or another, the DM is going to describe the route you should take to filling this need. The questions and comments made by the DM during the interview draw you a map. Let's look at those earlier remarks to see what they were really saying:

"You do not have much experience in selling fine jewelry."
"Can you make me look good selling fine jewelry?"

"Have you ever audited a retail chain?"
"Can you make me look good auditing my stores?"

"How about experience in computer-aided design?"
"Can your computer-aided design skills make me look good?"

"Have you ever been involved in the manufacture of office furniture?"
"Can you make me look good building desks and files?"

"I see you are with a fast-food chain. Have you ever managed a gourmet restaurant?"
"Can you make me look good managing my gourmet restaurant?"

"I don't see anything here about investor relations."
"Can you make me look good working with our investors?"

"In our business, it is especially important to keep the bankers happy."
"Can you make me look good working with my bankers?"

"We have a very difficult quality problem."
"Can you make me look good by solving my quality problem?"

You know the need to be satisfied and the route to take as you sell your benefit backed by your features. You are ahead of the others who are trying to impress the DM with how great they are without having a specific focus on the need they are there to satisfy.

Sell Your Benefit and Features

Suppose you have a very special pen to sell. It has a platinum point and a price of $50. It contains about $20-worth of the rare metal in its tip. You could knock on doors from here to Saturn and not sell a single one. However, that platinum point gives the pen a unique capability. Platinum is impervious to corrosive effects, so your pen can write with acid. That's the benefit. Sell this benefit and anyone from here to Saturn who needs to engrave with acid can be a customer. The sales pitch is not "Buy my wonderful pen with the platinum point." It is "Buy my wonderful pen that can write with acid because of its platinum point." Sell the benefit backed up by the feature.

So what is the benefit that you have to sell?

Is it your Ph.D.? No, no, no, no.

Is it your supervisory skills? No, no, no, no.

Is it that you're a CPA? No, no, no, no.

Is it your Academy Award? No, no, no, no.

Let's try again. What is the benefit you have to sell?

MY ABILITY TO MAKE THE DECISION MAKER LOOK GOOD!

That's the right answer. You may go to the head of the class.

Many salespeople don't understand the differences between a benefit and a feature. Those who sell to the consumer do. Skim through the ads in a copy of *Better Homes and Gardens,* for instance. You will read lead-ins like these: "Sleep like a log," "Get $100 back," "Reduce your cholesterol," "Clean faster," "Lead a more fruitful life." All are benefits. Consumer advertisements make it clear what to buy, selling the benefits and going on to explain the features that make these benefits possible.

Now leaf through the advertisements in a magazine that serves a technical industry. You'll see that the technical people are prone to tout the wondrous features of their work with only the broadest suggestion of what it might do for the customer. You will read such words as: "Aeronautics, a continuing challenge," "Advanced materials enter a new era," "Technology so far out it will provide answers to big questions," "When accuracy counts, count on advanced technology," or simply, "Imagine. . . ."

In consumer ads, it is clear which products to buy and what the benefits will be. In the industrial ads, you will have to dig deep into the ad copy to find out what's being sold and even deeper to learn of its benefits. Sometimes the benefits are unclear or even absent.

Take a lead from the consumer people. You know the benefit you are going to sell. Don't plug your ability to manage cost accounting, but do explain that when you establish improved cost-control methods in the DM's division profits will increase just as they did for your last boss, who was given new responsibilities as a result. Remember, subtlety is not your objective. The job offer is. Decision Makers eat this stuff up.

Playing in Overtime

You are eye-to-eye with the Decision Maker (at a cost of some $600 per hour). Your phone calls, letters, and resumes have gotten you here. Think of the in-person interview as the overtime period in a basketball game. You have played a fine game and are tied with the other invited candidates at the end of regulation time. That great performance now amounts to nil. All that matters is how you play in the overtime.

This situation should be to your liking, because for the first time you can use your full power. Your responses to "opportunity questions" can turn potential negatives into positives. You can use the DM's firsthand description of the job to shoot at the right target. Careful listening will identify the correct route to satisfying the DM's need to look good. Areas of suspected weakness in your candidacy and areas of special importance to the DM will be identified so that you can backfill or emphasize as appropriate. You have eye contact and body language to read. You will be onstage selling your benefit while the others stand there extolling their excellence.

In my judgment, 80 percent of the game lies ahead. That is, 80 percent of the hiring decision is based on the in-person interview. Your education, functional expertise, and previous accomplishments were important because they got you here. They were your ticket into the arena. But now, as that teacher of mine said, "The end is the test," and your test is about to begin. Isn't it a great feeling to know that you are walking in to the test well prepared?

Just to be absolutely sure that you are prepared, write the following on another 3 × 5 card to carry with you on interview day:

> "I am here to sell myself and get the job offer. The benefit I bring is my ability to make the Decision Maker look good. This benefit is backed by features— the ways in which I have done this for previous bosses."

Here you fill in specific examples of past performances that apply to your particular target at this interview, for instance:

- Your cost savings in final assembly that earned bonuses for the whole department.
- The ad you wrote that won the Higgly Award, which your boss accepted at the annual awards ceremony.
- Your revision of shipping procedures that eliminated late deliveries, as a result of which your department head was promoted.

No, you're not going to whip this card out and read it either. But you will know it's there, where it will help keep your objective and plan well in mind.

145

Chapter 13

Interview Tactics and Techniques

"Listen carefully to the words of the Decision Maker, and you will be led down the pathway to the job offer."

The DM is going to ask you questions aimed at determining how well you would do at making him or her look good. These questions are of three types.

- General: "Tell me about yourself."
- Doubt: "I do not see anything about our type of product in your background."
- Emphasis: "Tell me more about your work with the type of clients we sell to."

The General Question

This is the easy one. You simply deliver your prepared response. You have worked on it as you would on a speech to the alumni about your scaling of Mount Everest. You are even carrying prepared cue cards in your purse or pocket as subliminal prompts. You have based your presentation of yourself on the research you have done on the company and the Decision Maker. Your "speech" sells your benefit, backed by specific features in your background that apply to this particular situation.

Remember Ralph Miller, the financial specialist who decided to explore a job change when his company was acquired by a Swiss firm? We saw how he established his new job target: general management of an electronics manufacturing or computer company. He has kept the tools and pathways busy and is now onstage at an interview. The Decision Maker, Martin Ellis, has asked the classic general question, "Tell me about yourself," and Ralph has done his homework and prepared his speech:

> "Mr. Ellis, as I told you on the phone, I am a business analyst with Keystone Financial Services. I am basically a recovery-plan specialist. The company has been acquired by a Swiss firm and I anticipate considerable upheaval. This is a good time for me to consider a career change.
>
> "You will recall that my B.A. is from Drexel and my M.B.A. from Princeton. I am also a CPA. I've been with Keystone for fifteen years and am presently a vice president. The clients I serve are banks or other investors with interests in companies that are in difficulty. I go to these troubled organizations, analyze their problems, and devise a recovery plan. In some instances, I move in and manage an operation until it is on the road to recovery and new management can take over. Keystone is paid a fee plus stock in the company. I share in both.
>
> "You may be familiar with All Wright Construction and Engineering. Three years ago it was on the verge of bankruptcy as a result of a serious cash-flow problem. They had a fine reputation for quality work and a strong customer base, but the management had become distracted by racing sloops, golf games, world travel, and so on. The day-to-day administration of the company was a shambles. I moved in as general manager, turned the company around, and then handed it over to the management that I had hired and trained.
>
> "I responded to your advertisement for a general manager because I have performed successfully in that role many times. My last assignment was at McCabe Appliances. Since they are one of your main competitors, you will know that their chain of fourteen stores was going downhill rapidly. Since my intervention, they are climbing back up.
>
> "These successful turnarounds have made my management very happy, since all our fees are based on profit performance. My work added many extra dollars to the management bonus pool.
>
> "Before Keystone I spent three years as a broker with Paine Webber and before that three years as an accountant with Arthur Young. I am married and have three children. Mr. Ellis, what else can I tell you?"

Mr. Ellis can and probably will ask many more questions. One of them will certainly be:

"Mr. Miller, how much money do you want?"

"Mr. Ellis, the important consideration for me right now is career path. I am looking for an opportunity where I can share more fully in the results of my labors. When I turn a company around for Keystone, I do share in the gains when the stock price rises. However, I believe my rewards would be much greater as a member of an operating company like yours."

"How much are you making now?"

"My base salary is in six figures."

We will return to the question of salary, along with many other points concerning the interview, at the appropriate time. But for now, we must return to selling your benefit.

The Doubt Question

Jennifer Rhodes, you will remember, has been a successful buyer in jewelry for a department store and wants to move into field sales of dental products. Her interviewer asks the doubt question:

"Ms. Rhodes, your background does not seem to include much experience in dentistry."

This is a signal for Jennifer to backfill and cover what is perceived as an important void in her experience.

"Ms. Wade, now that you mention it, that is an area of my background I should have expanded on in my resume. My minor in college was health care, which included many courses relevant to dentistry. My first job after college was with an orthodontist. He was a great teacher, and I learned a lot from him. In fact, he tried to convince me to go to dental school. He was pleased that my way with people brought him many new patients, and he felt I would do very well in the profession. Believe me, I have a good foundation in dental products."

The Emphasis Question

One of the accomplishments John Allard listed when he set his job goals was the establishment of a communications program that helped convince his company's employees that a union was not needed there. Now he is asked by his interviewer:

> "Mr. Allard, tell me about your experience dealing with the union question."

This tells John that the matter of union relations is of prime importance in the position he is interviewing for.

> **"Mr. Beauchamp, I developed a communications program at Logan Laboratories that was credited with convincing the employees that a union was not necessary. It was a positive campaign that boosted the company rather than discrediting the union. We took very positive steps and were always careful to respect management-labor relationships and the labor law. This enabled my boss to spend his time running a smooth business instead of wrangling with union leaders."**

Listen

Listen carefully to the words of the Decision Maker, and you will be led down the pathway to the job offer. Whether the questions ask about you in a general way, express doubt about your experience, or place emphasis on certain areas of your background, direct your responses to satisfying the needs you find expressed there. Describe your past performance and tie it in with success experienced by your boss.

- "added many extra dollars to the management bonus pool."
- "brought him many new patients . . ."
- "enabled my boss to spend his time running a smooth business . . ."

Note that the candidate's success is almost incidental. DMs thrive on this treatment, and what's good for the DM is good for your shot at the job offer.

Interruptions

Interviews are subject to interruption from various quarters: the telephone, the secretary, the boss, and others. You have the right to get the meeting back on your track, but you must have the skill to do so. As was spelled out earlier, you have a sizable investment in your time with the DM.

The telephone can be the worst offender. If the DM has left instructions that no calls be put through while the interview is in progress, this is a strong indication that the open position is an important one. On one of the occasions when I should have walked out, a manager let me sit like a duffel bag of old laundry while he had a half-hour telephone conversation about a computer printout with one of his division managers. If something similar happens to you, walk out. If the meeting is interrupted by several shorter phone calls, it is perfectly proper to ask that calls be held. If, after you have made this request, the calls are still not held, you are probably wasting your time. Don't be a "people pleaser" and just sit there. Don't be bashful. Walk out.

Secretaries can call the DM on the intercom or barge in to the room. Treat this as you would phone interruptions. The boss, on the other hand, can do what he or she wants, including interrupting at any time and often. The DM has no control over this. Don't try to fight it. Spouses or relatives of the DM can be in the same category as bosses, so don't try to fight them either.

If the interview has been interrupted, get back on the track by picking up the conversation where it left off, if it was moving toward your objective, or by resuming the discussion in a direction that will.

Suppose you are describing how your special computer programming technique made it possible for a company's new software package to be sold for 15 percent less than the nearest competing system. You are on the verge of springing the clincher that sells your benefit—how your manager's section was given the responsibility for all new-product development as a result—when the DM's boss walks in and demands to know who had the nerve to park in his parking space. After the crisis is past, you say:

> **"We were talking about the free-lance work I did for CrashPruf Computers. I was about to point out that the president thanked me personally. The extra profit resulting from my work enabled him to report an additional 2 cents per share in his annual report to the stockholders. I know I could help your company. Do you think it would be best to install the same work-flow procedures I established for CrashPruf or to improve what you already have in place?"**

On the other hand, if you need to reorient the interview and are thankful for the interruption and the chance to cut off the interviewer's account of her last flight on *Concorde*, try with something like this:

"Ms. Sharpe, which do you consider to be the most valuable experience for this position, my work as a free lance or my time with the agency?"

No Decision Maker who is serious about filling a position can fail to respond to this change of direction.

Digressions

Digressions can be much more serious than simple interruptions. This is true whether they are spawned by the interviewer or, ridiculous as the idea may seem, by you.

The self-made expert seems to have only a slight tendency to wander off the course of the interview to brag or reminisce. The professional manager always stays on track. It's the inexperienced interviewer who is most prone to try to impress the candidate or tell war stories.

Your interview time is valuable, and you must keep the meeting on track. If the interviewer has gone off on a tangent, describing his restoration of a 1944 Mercury coupe, you are not moving toward your objective. You could say, "I'm really not interested in your junk car. Let's talk about how great you will look when you hire me." But you'd be advised not to. This is the time to use some of that subtlety you have been hoarding.

"I certainly appreciate the importance of a diversion like restoring cars. My diversion is sailing. I need to get away from time to time and do some quiet thinking. In fact, the idea for the ad campaign that won my company the Grabber Award came to me while I was relaxing on the Ookalaca River. Do you think a similar campaign would boost your sales, or do your products require a more structured treatment?"

But the digression does not always come from the Decision Maker. Take the candidate Mr. Runoffatthemouth. He is abruptly clouted by the realization that he is trying to show how great he is by telling the story of his rescue of a diving buddy at 90 feet. There is no way back, but he can cut the detour short and return to a more direct route to the job offer:

"Scuba is a diversion that helps me sort out my thoughts about work. Two months ago on the 3-hour ride back from Catalina I sketched out the design that won the redecoration

contract for the Art Center. My boss has been named to head
the project. Your company is strong in both new construction
and refurbishing. Where do you think my background will fit
best?"

By allowing the conversation to sink 90 feet below the surface of
the Pacific Ocean, Mr. Runoffatthemouth nearly sank his chances
at the job, too. He caused expensive interview time to be wasted on
useless chatter when he should have been selling his benefit.

One last word on digressions, however—damaging as they can
be, there is a case to be made for letting a Decision Maker wander in
the direction of self-praise. Everyone enjoys a good listener. After
sitting beside Ambassador Weston-Smith at the annual banquet of
the International Underprivileged Children's Relief Fund, a
woman reported:

"I've never been near an important person like the
Ambassador. He is the most impressive person I have ever
met. He let me talk about myself all night."

If you sense that the DM wants a good listener, be one. It can be an
important part of the "look-good" strategy. However, don't rely on
that tactic alone. Strike a balance and keep things moving toward
your goal.

A Test

You are all salespeople, right? You are trained in selling yourself
to Decision Makers. The secrets of the assumptive close, the choice
question, and benefits and features have been revealed to you.
Now, here is a test question. How many choice questions were there
in the preceding examples of tactics for handling interruptions
and digressions? Right you are. There were four.

"Do you think it would be best to install the same work-flow
procedures I established for CrashPruf or to improve what you
already have in place?"

"Ms. Sharpe, which do you consider to be the most valuable
experience for this position, my work as a free lance or my
time with the agency?"

"Do you think a similar campaign would boost your sales, or
do your products require a more structured treatment?"

"Your company is strong in both new construction and refurbishing. Where do you think my background would fit best?"

Negative Polarity

Negative polarity is more or less easy to identify. The DM may refer openly to areas in which your qualifications seem questionable. Repeated questions directed at or around a particular aspect of your experience may give you a clue. Lack of response to your touting of specific accomplishments is also a hint.

If the Decision Maker seems to zero in on a negative element in your candidacy, you have three choices. You can attempt to correct the unfavorable impression, switch to a more favorable subject, or walk out.

Perhaps you can correct a negative impression by expanding on your accomplishments in the questionable area, emphasizing the way they helped your organization and boss. If, however, the disputed area does not seem to be of particular importance, switch to a positive subject:

"That program did not go well for me, but I have applied the lessons learned to my present work. The new campaign that I instituted has increased savings accounts by 12 percent in less than four months. Would my experience be best applied in conducting a similar campaign for you, or would you prefer to move out in a new direction?"

In the case of an obvious impasse, like the one between me and the fireplug, politely end the standoff and leave. Otherwise it's going to be like trying to barbecue on wet charcoal: you'll be eating cold sandwiches in the end, so you might as well put a stop to the hassle early.

Paraphrasing

Another way of keeping the interview moving toward the job offer is to paraphrase the DM's remarks, either to emphasize a positive or to erase a negative.

"Ms. Mason, when you mentioned my work at Madison's Department Store, I was pleased to find that you knew of my success with the Tanton watches. Tanton was a new company without an established track record, but my evaluation was

> that the product was good and that the company could and
> would meet its delivery commitments. The line was a hit and
> was essentially exclusively ours for a year."

This paraphrase brings a favorable subject back onstage, provides
an opportunity to add to your features, and drives home your benefit.

In the following example, the paraphrase brings a negative back
on the scene, where it can be quashed. Of course, not all of us can
have official secrecy to hide behind, but I'm sure we can think of
something just as good when the occasion demands.

> "Mr. Kline, you mentioned the report in the trade press that
> Project Eller was late and seriously overspent. You know I am
> Project Leader. I feel compelled to comment, because what
> may appear to you to be a failure is in reality an exciting
> success. That article discussed the original contract price and
> scope of work without knowledge of the major redirection
> and increased funding that resulted from an engineering
> breakthrough. Unfortunately the details are classified, but I
> assure you that Project Eller is well on track and within its
> revised budget. In fact, for our work on the project, my boss
> has just been promoted to Division Engineer, and I have
> moved up a notch."

Infinite Variations

Infinite variations in emphasis, every sort of pitfall, all the nu-
ances imaginable can materialize in the course of an in-person
interview. No handbook can predict and handle them all. Be convinced that you *can*, however, and much better than anyone else in
the race. Your work in the early rounds has earned you a place
among the other finalists, but your continuing efforts have set you
apart. You have detailed knowledge of the target company and the
Decision Maker. You are ready to respond to the "tell me about
yourself" question. You are going to ask the DM to explain the
position so you can aim your artillery effectively.

You understand the Decision Maker's code and how to sell the
benefit. You have anticipated critical questions, know how to recover from interruptions, have skill in using the assumptive close
and choice question, and can manage negative polarity. You are
way ahead of the pack but not quite ready to dive in and race across
the interview pool doing the Australian crawl, not without the
all-important discussion of salary.

The Salary Question

You've heard me say it before: NEVER, NEVER, NEVER answer the question "How much money do you want?" Now it's going to be etched wherever your etched items reside. Do not mention money on your resume, in your responses to ads, or at the interview. (The exception is when you are working with headhunters.) If you answer the question, you will probably price yourself out of the competition or wind up with considerably less than you might have gotten. It is statistically improbable that you can pick a figure that is exactly right. And you want them to want you before they price you.

I always bought my suits from John. As soon as I walked into the store, he would grab a suit coat for me to try on, never letting me look at the price. Invariably I would end up buying a suit of that make. Invariably it would be one of his higher-priced models. His ploy was to get me into a suit coat that looked and felt good first. Sure, I would go through the routine of trying on the cheaper labels, but I would always return to the top of the line. If I had looked at the price first, I might never have considered it. I thank John for not letting me look at the price. I always felt well dressed.

Don't let the Decision Maker see your price tag until it has been decided that you are the one for the job. Otherwise he or she might be deprived of your benefit, shying away from what seemed at first to be a high cost. The DM who has come to recognize your value will be pleased to pay the price.

The salary question must be an automatic trigger, and your response must be Pavlovian:

"Ms. Liggett, the important consideration for me at this point is my career and the opportunity this position will give me to make a contribution to your organization. You represent a reasonable company, and I am sure you will make a reasonable offer if we both feel this is the right job for me."

At this point, the interviewer may press for a figure. Finally you may be asked for your present salary. Always answer in terms of your *base* pay. Do not mention any bonuses or incentives or perquisites. These can be valuable negotiation points to be used in arriving at your compensation package. Don't waste them now.

If the thought strikes you that a good negotiating ploy would be to inflate your present pay in order to maximize your next compensation package, don't! Or be prepared for this:

"Mr. Armstrong, please bring a copy of your last pay stub when you start work on Monday."

"Sorry, I'm a liar. I didn't earn as much as I said. I'll have to go work for someone else."

Don't snicker. I actually had this happen with a candidate before I learned to make the warning part of my standard instructions.

Some of you already may have decided that you are not going to reveal your present pay under *any* circumstances. You want to be paid what you are worth to the new company, and that should be independent of what you are making now. Cancel plans to shoot for that orbit. You won't get off the launchpad. Write this in your hat along with the other notes: the new company will have to know what you made at your last job or you won't be hired. Don't fight it. If you refuse to tell, all the new company has to do is ask your old company. And if the new company can't find out, it will just move on to the next candidate.

Since you most likely will not be made an offer during the first interview, we will discuss what to do when this happens in a later chapter. For now, we want to concentrate on getting that offer rather than on reacting to getting it.

Ask for the Offer

The interview is winding down. The DM's body language tells you so. There may even be glances at the clock. It is time to get off the stage . . . but not before you ask for an offer.

John Allard senses that the interview is over and says:

"Mr. Elton, you have given me a very good picture of the position and its importance to the company. It is work I like to do and can do well. I know I am the right person for the job. If you feel the same way, I would like to have you make me an offer."

At this point, Allard does not know whether he really wants the job or not. *He does want the offer.* Otherwise, all the work he has done to get here has been for nothing. At this point, Mr. Elton may not know whether he wants to make an offer or not. However, he is convinced that John wants the offer, and that is a positive sign.

I often run into candidates who are reluctant to interview for an attractive position because they are not sure they would take the job if it were offered. They feel they would be flying under false colors.

When I remind them that they will not be the only person interviewed, they realize that agreeing to an interview does not commit them to accepting an offer any more than it commits the company to making one. I then suggest that having agreed to play the game, they should play to win, part of which is asking for the job offer.

Up until the moment the offer is made, the ball is in the company's court. Without the offer, all you have done is meet a few nice people and maybe enjoy a plane ride and a couple of expense-account meals. With the offer in hand, the ball is in your court. Now you can ask all those questions about perks and benefits and do all kinds of in-depth fact finding from employees, former employees, customers, and competitors. Then you make up your mind.

The Action Step

John Allard ends the meeting with an action step:

"Mr. Elton, thank you for your time. I will be very pleased to receive a job offer from you. I will call you on Friday to follow up, but if you feel that is too early, how would Monday be?"

The follow-up step is established, and I'm sure you noticed it was done with a choice question.

There is another follow-up step almost too obvious to mention, but, just to be on the safe side, here it is. It is the follow-up letter. I am not calling it a "thank-you note," because it shouldn't be.

Dear Mr. Elton:

I am very enthusiastic about the position we discussed. The more I consider the many points we covered, the more I am convinced that I am the one for the job. I hope you feel the same way and will make me an offer.

I enjoyed our meeting and appreciate the time you took with me. I'll call Monday to follow up.

Sincerely,

John Allard

In Chapter 17, we will return to the DM's office and discuss what happens once the offer is made, including how to negotiate salary, perks, and other terms of employment. But first, a few words about achieving poise and the ultimate in preparedness through practice.

Chapter 14

Practice Makes Perfect

"Fit your preparation to the value of the prize."

I probably don't need to tell you to dress right for the interview. If you're not sure how to dress, learn. There are several popular books on the subject. Or look at appropriate magazines and style yourself after the businesspeople you see there. Pay particular attention to your shoes. Don't think you can polish up the ones you wear for gardening and make them presentable.

Don't carry a briefcase full of resumes or letters of reference. It would be a useless prop and a distraction to you and the DM. Leave it in the car.

Don't smoke. Even if the DM does, don't. Smoking is another needless distraction. Where will you put the ashes, for instance?

Refuse the offer of coffee. It is only an annoyance. What will you do when you find that you've put a ring on the mahogany desk or you can't put your shaking hand out of sight because you're holding the coffee cup?

Avoid interviews over lunch or dinner. As mentioned earlier, a restaurant is a ghastly environment in which to try and win a job offer. Both the interviewer and the interviewee are distracted by the food, interrupted by the waiters, and hampered by the lack of privacy. But if you can't avoid a lunch or dinner meeting, at least order something that is easy to manipulate. Stay away from live Maine lobsters, barbecued spareribs, and so on. Do not drink at all, or be very careful to follow the DM's lead. This can be difficult, since the DM may be waiting to see what you do as part of the interview process. If you feel any doubt about the DM's position, decline a drink. If you say, "yes," you may wind up drinking alone and under the DM's scrutiny. But if your DM is the sort who won't take "no" for an answer, order a drink and let it sit untouched.

I once saw this carried off with great savoir faire. I was in Moscow in connection with an international oil symposium. A group of us were invited to spend the day as guests of the USSR Minister of Petroleum, cruising on a state-owned yacht over the waterways that encircle the city. The Russians served a sumptuous meal, as usual washed down with copious amounts of vodka. The Syrian Minister of Petroleum, a strict teetotaler by religion and perhaps even by state edict, was at my table. I watched him with interest over the course of the meal as at least fifteen toasts were proposed. He would stand with the rest of us, raise his glass to his lips with gusto, and never sip a drop. And if the others noticed his little deception, they never mentioned it.

Don't even think of carrying your beeper. Or if you do, also take your cellular phone, your briefcase computer with modem, and your portable fax. The DM may want someone who has good connections.

If I have to say anything about chewing gum, one of us is in the wrong line.

Poise

Lots of books about interviewing tell you to avoid sweaty palms. I was never quite sure how to do that. Maybe there was a secret no one would share with me, like rubbing in talc or bowing toward Antarctica and praying to the Great God Cool. But relax. The real antidote for sweaty palms is poise. You are going into your in-person interview with a high poise quotient because of the preparations you have made. You will not be one of those who have to depend on ad-libs.

I've made some good speeches in my day and some bad ones. The bad ones occurred when I approached them too casually or was overly concerned. The good ones happened when the adrenaline was flowing in anticipation but was tempered with a touch of casualness. The same is true of interviews. You want to be excited but not panicked, relaxed but not laid back.

In my dim and distant past, the U.S. Army Air Corps was screening Reserve officers for Regular commissions. A college buddy really wanted to get back into uniform, and he asked me to drive him to Boston for his evaluation since I had the only car that ran at the time, a 1930 Model A Ford. When we got there, I decided to go through the screening rather than just sit around. Unlike my friend with his fiery desire, I was very casual about it, or I was until my turn to be interviewed by the board of seven Air Corps colonels. The guy before me had come out with his tail between his legs. My adrenaline started to flow as I walked in and sat down in the hot seat facing the semicircle of inquisitors. As a lieutenant, I had very little experience of being in the presence of a full colonel, let alone seven of them at once. None of them spoke. They just stared. I stared back, starting at one end of the row and locking eyes with each one in turn. During my second pass, the one who seemed to be in charge said, "Lieutenant, would you like a cigarette?" and offered me one with as many holes in it as a clarinet. I guess that was supposed to fluster me, but I covered the holes with my fingers, smoked, and returned their stares. And when they began their questioning, we got along very well. Six months after the screening, telegrams went out to the winners. One in every sixteen applicants made it. I was one of them.

I have always felt that on that occasion I struck just the right balance between adrenaline and calm. Since then I have been striving to reach that same balance for speeches, interviews, and similar performances. Frankly, I have never done as well since, but at least the incident has set a standard for me to strive toward.

A Practice Jump

In parachuting, the student jumps from a 10-foot-high platform before taking the first real jump from a plane at 3,000 feet. Wouldn't it be nice if you could do the same with interviews? If you are a member of Forty-Plus, you will have practice interviews. If you are in outplacement, you may. Some search firms include interview drills among their services. And even if you have none of these at your disposal, there are ways.

Practice interviews at Forty-Plus are conducted by the counseling committee. Each member must have at least one practice interview in order to graduate. The candidate is assigned a target company and position that fits his or her background and is given a couple of days in which to do the necessary research. The session is videotaped and is conducted by two graduate members. One acts as the DM, and the other sits in silence, taking notes. The interviewee is instructed to perform exactly as if the interview were real, starting with the knock on the office door.

I have gone through several Forty-Plus interview sessions, two before I graduated and four or five more as a member of the counseling committee. These were very valuable experiences to me, as both trainee and trainer. In every session, realism quickly displaced any feeling of playacting. The criticisms given were positive, not necessarily kind but always constructive. The video playback spoke eloquently to the candidate regarding posture, poise, eye contact, body language, etc. Some candidates were required by the counseling committee to have two or three practice interviews before they could graduate. Others asked for repeat sessions.

Here is a practice interview rating sheet that covers many of the points we have discussed. It is similar to the one used by Forty-Plus.

PRACTICE INTERVIEW RATING SHEET

Date _____

Interviewee _____

Counselor _____

Performance Element	Unsatisfactory	Satisfactory	Comments
Job Information Questions			
Tell Me About Yourself			
Opportunity Questions			
Needs/Benefits/Features			
Reorientations			
Paraphrasing			
Question/Answer/Talk Ratio			
Salary Questions			
Why You Left Your Job			
Ask for the Offer			
Action Step			
Social Graces			
Poise			

Constructive Criticism:

Practice with a Friend

If you are in the new-job struggle on your own, without the aid of Forty-Plus or outplacement, don't despair. Having a mock interview is as easy as asking a friend to meet with you. Choose the friend thoughtfully. He or she should be knowledgeable about your work and have a degree of sound judgment. If your target is a management position with an auto repair chain, don't pick a friend who can't check the air in her tires or, for that matter, a friend who's something of an airhead.

Provide this carefully chosen person with the list of "opportunity questions" ahead of time. Place special emphasis on these:

- "How much money do you want?"
- "Why did you leave your last job?"
- "Tell me about yourself."

Explain the importance of:

- Your request that the Decision Maker describe the position to you.
- Your request for an offer.
- Your close with an action step.

Provide a copy of the practice interview rating sheet and review it with your friend. Set a time and place for the interview. No, not at the poolside during happy hour. If an office is not available, use the local library. Dress in your interview outfit, right down to the tie you will wear or the purse you will carry. Impress your friend with the importance of the session and the significance of the areas to be covered. Describe the target company and the position. If you do not have such a target at the time of the interview, make one up.

When you meet, take full advantage of your friend's presence by covering all areas of the rating sheet. Give your answers to the critical "opportunity questions." Make your statements asking for the offer and establishing the action step. Find out how they sound. Probe the intricacies of the position with your colleague so you can identify linkups of your past experience with areas critical to performance in the new job. Try these linkups to see if your friend thinks they sell your benefit, displaying your ability to make the Decision Maker look good. Convince your friend to be honest with you, not kind, even when it concerns things of a personal nature, such as eye contact, posture, mannerisms, dress, and poise.

If you have had little or no interview experience, it is imperative that you arrange for practice. If you are apprehensive or rusty, organize warm-up sessions. Remind yourself of the importance, and cost, of your time with the Decision Maker, and you will make the effort. Analyze your helper's remarks and observations with care, and revise your presentation as necessary.

Another Way

Suppose you have an interview coming up that you think may be the gateway to the career opportunity of a lifetime. You want to do everything possible to come away with the prize. A realistic dry run can carry you a long way toward the goal by helping the real thing go off without a hitch.

In the early days of the missile business at Cape Canaveral, we would conduct dry runs to help the countdown go as smoothly as possible on launch day. The missiles and support gear were kept at what is now Kennedy Air Force Base and were hauled out to the Cape for the occasion, which resulted in a sizable parade of equipment through the heart of Cocoa Beach. Our dry runs could include just about everything except pushing the firing button, but one day I had the term emphatically redefined for me.

At that time, I was a first lieutenant, and the place was still called JLRPG, for Joint Long-Range Proving Ground. It was manned by personnel from the Army, Navy, Marines, and Air Force, all intermingled and all outranking me. I had read the book about space flight by Willie Ley and another about rockets, which made me an expert compared to the others, regardless of rank. For this reason, I had been made Propulsion Officer and Firing Officer. A U.S. Army colonel was Ground Safety Officer.

On the day in question, the dry run was going without a hitch, that is until the colonel explained that his definition of "dry" was quite different from mine. I had included in the parade to the Cape propellant trucks loaded with liquid fuel and oxidizer. Since, according to his definition, a dry run meant no dangerous liquids to contend with, he had left his fire trucks and emergency crews at the base. He snapped me to attention and chewed me out in a loud voice until both our throats were dry. I had to stay at the Cape and wait for his fire trucks to come and escort my propellant trucks home. They showed up sometime after midnight.

You can arrange a realistic dry run that can come very close to "pushing the button." Call on another friend and ask him or her to arrange a mock interview for you. This means asking your friend to cash in some chips with another friend on your behalf. You should not know the third person, and the third person should not know you. Let's call him Paul King. King should be prepared just as your friend was in the previous case, but this preparation is all done through the intermediary. King does not have your resume but knows as much about your background as a DM would who had granted you an interview.

You arrive at King's office, wait for your appointment, and walk in and introduce yourself, all as if it were a real interview.

When the meeting is over, King uses the practice interview rating sheet to appraise your performance. He gives particular attention to the "constructive criticism" block. Since he is not acquainted with you, he will be more objective than a friend.

Still Another Way

There is another way to get practice of sorts. It is through so-called "information interviewing."

"Mr. Beam, I have called you because I am considering making a career change, and one of the paths I am considering is contract negotiations, a field in which you are an acknowledged expert. Could I have a few minutes of your time to learn more about what you do and what you consider to be the opportunities in your field?"

Such a meeting will help you gain poise, give you a chance to wear your interview clothes, and provide practice in other aspects of interviewing. Some theorists in the field of job search recommend this as a path to a new job, suggesting that your asking questions will make you so attractive you will be hired. For my money, if finding a new position is your objective, the information interview is an impractical approach. It's sort of like cutting bait when you ought to be bailing.

If, on the other hand, you have long-range plans to move into a new career field, an information interview can be very helpful. You will find that the people you approach are flattered by your request and glad to share what they know. Information interviews have a definite place in the job hunts of "freshouts" ("fresh out" of high school or college), and they will be discussed in detail in a later chapter.

How important the need for practice is to you will depend on your urgency factor and your level on the career ladder. Those with no money worries will undoubtedly be content to wing it—why scuttle a good thing through irresponsible preparation? But the rest of you will want to fit your preparation to the value of the prize.

Chapter 15

References

"Select your references with all the care you would use in choosing a scuba buddy. You want someone you know won't cut off your life support."

If you think the business of picking references is simple, wipe that file and enter new data. In the olden days (pre-1970s, by my calendar) this was a rather routine task. You simply picked out a few people you thought would say nice things about you. Today it is much more complicated. First, just thinking that nice things will be said no longer makes it so. It's a jungle out there. Second, the activities of the legal eagles have made the jungle even more perilous. The combination of the two makes the task of selecting references a safari that must be properly guided. Put on your pith helmet, and we will forge ahead together.

Unfriendly References

Many years ago, I was interviewed by a large industrial firm in Los Angeles. I was not convinced I wanted the job, but I did want the offer, which looked pretty certain. The clinching lunch, where the president was to introduce me to my new peers, was all arranged. When I arrived, expecting to bask in my triumph, it was obvious that my plug had been pulled. Instead of lunch with the staff at the California Club, the president snuck me off to Joe's Chophouse and explained they were still checking references. I never heard from him again.

Some detective work on my part, greatly aided by the work of an accomplice inside the company, revealed that one of my references had stabbed me. He had been my controller for the two years I was busy turning a sick company into a winner. We had survived some interesting crises together, and I never suspected for even a microsecond that he was anything but a staunch backer. I will never know exactly why he did me in or just what type of knife he used, but it was clear he had gone for my throat. This story emphasizes the point that you must be very sure of the people you select to comment on your capabilities.

Legal Eagles

Suppose that Alec Reasoner has interviewed Peter Fulton and wants to check his references. One of them is Will Hessler at Orion Developers. The scenario can develop in one of several directions:

- Hessler may give a glowing recommendation.
- Peter may have it all wrong, and his "friend" Hessler may plunge the knife.
- Hessler may be fearful of repercussions from whatever he says, and so may decline to say anything.

Legal influences on the business of choosing and using references add to an already sporty course. The current legal system encourages the proliferation of people who will take any case that has any chance of producing a fee at any time. This makes it mandatory that you develop specific skills in the handling of references.

The Risk of a Glowing Report

What risk can there be, you wonder, in Will Hessler giving a glowing account of Peter Fulton? The risk comes into it if Peter bombs out on the job because of faults Hessler neglected to cover and some hungry lawyer convinces the "victimized" company to sue Hessler and company. Don't chuckle. This is a real threat. Suppose Hessler knows that Peter is under Grand Jury indictment for embezzlement and neglects to mention it. Later Peter goes off to jail. One of the legal scavengers would snap up the case in a flash, and even the more principled practitioners might consider it a good case in favor of the new employer. This threat of legal backlash can turn an otherwise positive reference into a refusal to comment.

The Backstab

If Hessler plunges the knife in Peter's back, Hessler can again be sued. Under the Freedom of Information Act, Peter is entitled to a copy of any written recommendation concerning him, and, through the deposition process, he can have access to the content of any verbal appraisal. Unless Hessler has well-documented evidence to substantiate his negative comments regarding Peter, he will lose. On the California scene, for example, such libel suits are decided in the plaintiff's favor about 75 percent of the time. This would seem to protect a candidate from the derogatory remarks of references, but *don't drop your guard.* If someone is out to get you, he or she will find a way.

Nolo Contendere

"Nolo contendere" is Latin and legal for "I do not wish to contend," and the current legal climate drives the majority of would-be references toward "nolo" responses. You may think it's Safe City for you when a person is fearful of giving a reference and refuses to say anything, good or bad. It isn't. An innocent "nolo" from an apprehensive advocate can be interpreted as a thumbs-down.

A California legal eagle (or should I say condor?) is now suing a Fortune 500 company on behalf of an employee who was fired. The suit is based on the fact that one of the company's top managers pleaded "nolo" when asked for a reference, the contention being that this was in effect a negative comment that hindered the employee in his search for a new position. As already indicated, California statistics predict that the plaintiff will win, which in this case would be unjust. I know the situation, because the "nolo" comment was made to me. The manager chose to say nothing rather than report justifiable negatives about the ex-employee. In fact, he was trying to help rather than hinder.

Forget References?

Knowing all this, do you still want to use references? Certainly. Even in the current legal environment, where many companies have a policy of "no comment," you cannot avoid reference checks entirely. Your role is to make certain that everyone contacted for a recommendation will bolster your campaign.

There are four types of possible references:

- Associates you can be *absolutely sure* are genuine advocates.
- Personnel you can't avoid, although you suspect they would like to be members of your firing squad.
- The "nolo contendere" crowd.
- Personnel who would like to fire the bullets but only have blanks.

Map the Jungle

The first thing to do is define your world of possible references. This includes the group you would like to use, as well as those who will be used whether you like it or not. Make two lists. The group of your choosing is relatively easy, but remember, select your references with all the care you would use in choosing a scuba buddy. You want someone you know won't cut off your life support. Three is a good number. Too many more and it will appear that you're trying to paint over blemishes.

The list of unavoidables will be more difficult to compile. Obviously, it must contain the names of your last three bosses. Then it becomes time to ponder. Consider listing other key associates in your last three companies. Having listened attentively to the words of the Decision Maker, try to predict others the DM will ask for or ferret out without asking. Anything you have learned about his or her old school ties, church groups, social clubs, or previous employment may give you clues.

Now decide which references you will provide, though you will provide them only when asked and only at the proper time. Pick three of your own choice and three from the unavoidable list. (Of course, the same name or names can appear on both lists.) Generally, a DM will contact up to three people when checking references. When someone in the personnel department is given the task, many more may be interrogated. (Remember the Personnel Canon: "Look for a flaw. A vacancy is better than a flawed incumbent, even if the work remains undone.")

The Proper Use of References

Notice that I said in the previous paragraph, "Now decide which references you will provide, though you will provide them only when asked and *only at the proper time.*" Use your references only when it is evident that the Decision Maker has genuine interest. This means that you definitely don't list them on your resume. Neither do you provide them to the personnel department unless it is absolutely necessary in order to move forward and you consider the position worth it.

You want to avoid the pestering of your key contacts. Too many inquiries can end up creating a negative environment, and by the time *the* job is at hand a supportive reference may have turned antagonistic. By definition, the names you have selected are important in their field, and there are many out there who might use the excuse of checking references to talk to these people for self-serving purposes and at your expense.

Use your references sparingly . . . and only when it really counts. The proper role of references is to confirm that you are what you have said you are, and the ideal time to deploy them is *after you have been selected.* If pressed to supply names earlier, politely explain that your references are important resources and you are not going to involve them in dry runs.

References are not to be used to convince the Decision Maker of how great you are. Remember, this is not what the DM really cares about. References should be used to substantiate your claims of being able to make the Decision Maker look good.

Calibration

Think about the tone of the responses you expect your possible references to give and separate them into the Knowns and the Unknowns. Scrutinize your list of Knowns, and if you sense a flicker of doubt, move the suspect name to the list of Unknowns. The Knowns may also include people you are sure will give negative inputs. But move them over to the Unknowns, because the ammunition they will use is unknown to you. Then investigate every name on your Unknowns list to find out exactly what response each will give when asked about you.

This is not difficult. Select a trusted friend who has a flare for intrigue and a convincing telephone style. Have this friend call each Unknown. Here are two examples:

"Mr. Davis, this is Rob Veller of National Distributors. I am interested in Ralph Miller, who is going to be considered for employment as general manager. He worked for you for four years. The need is for someone who knows the market for industrial switches. Do you consider him a viable candidate?"

"Ms. Spinner, I am Beverly Mentor of Worthmore Advertising. Lynn Longmyer is going to receive serious evaluation as a customer service specialist. She tells us that she worked for you for five years. Do you consider her to be a likely candidate?"

Note that these inquiries contain no falsehoods. Neither Mr. Veller nor Ms. Spinner said the candidate was being considered for a job with them. This type of call will produce results. Your friend will be able to separate the white hats from the black hats for you.

You may be unable to recruit a friend who is gregarious enough. However, for those with a sufficiently high urgency factor or level on the career ladder, there is another avenue. Ads frequently appear in such newspapers as the *New York Times* and the *Wall Street Journal* offering reference checking services for a fee. If you have doubts about people who are likely to be asked to provide references for you and the career target is a valuable one, the cost of these services will be worth it.

Program the White Hats

Now that you've identified the white hats, you want to upgrade their potential contributions from simple references to testimonials or even full commercial messages. You do this by programming them on what to say when the time comes. Use the same technique you applied when enlisting friends and associates to become additional eyes and ears in support of your job search. Remember? You wrote them a letter.

Here is a sample of the process applied to the programming of a reference:

May 27, 1990

Mr. Robert T. Witters
President
Sepulveda Venture Capital, Inc.
Suite 4505
1901 Avenue of the Stars
Century City, CA 90067

Dear Mr. Witters:

Thank you for letting me use you as a reference.

I am being considered for the General Manager position at Elliot Marine. George Lane, the Chairman of the Board, needs someone who can move in quickly, find out what is wrong, and turn the place around.

You will recall that I did a similar job for your company when I moved into Abbot Industrial Supply and put it back in the black in less than a year. I brought in Carl Gibbs as the new General Manager, and I understand that you are very pleased with him.

I'm sure you will also remember that I brought Bradford Metals out of bankruptcy in a much shorter time than anyone thought was possible.

I expect that Mr. Lane will call you. I will appreciate it if you see fit to comment on my ability.

Sincerely,

Ralph Miller

The letter puts words in Mr. Witters's mind and, Ralph hopes, in his mouth. It also points out how Ralph made Witters look good.

Handle the Black Hats

You have made the effort to distinguish the good guys from the bad guys. If there is a firing squad, you know who will be on it and the caliber of bullet they will fire if given the chance. There is but one thing left to do. Get them first.

Sally, a key vice president, has been called in by the president and told that she is fired. Evaluations of her background, experience, and accomplishments show that she is well qualified and has performed exceptionally well. When she looks for a new job, Sally can try to cover up her firing by stating that she left "by mutual agreement" or "out of a desire for more opportunity," but she knows that, when asked, the president will respond with a negative evaluation like the following (how else can top managers justify such actions?):

> "She is a very nice person, but frankly I don't think she ever got on top of her job. Every time I needed her it seemed she was not around. Besides, I think there was a lack of communication between us."

Sally knows she was fired because she was not in the daily lineup of those waiting to massage the boss's ego. Instead, she worked to achieve an 18 percent sales increase. Sally's career prospects, earning power, and general well-being are threatened by the boss's potential to make negative remarks, which would only be thinly disguised attempts at bolstering an inflated ego. Under the circumstances, Sally is justified in striking first. Her only course is to admit that she was fired and to discredit the one who fired her before she is discredited herself. Sally can say:

> **"Ms. Tinker, I know you will want to check with Marge Mittick, my boss at Murdock Electric. She fired me. Now I realize that I should have quit earlier, but the challenge of exceeding the sales forecast by 18 percent kept me going. And I was hesitant to believe what seems obvious now, that I could never be successful there as long as I was unwilling to take a number and join those waiting to massage her ego every day."**

Turn your creativity loose and get before you are gotten. But make sure you have a valid foundation for the weapons you use. Don't suggest that the boss manipulated the books—and knew you knew it—unless, of course, you can prove it.

How About the "Nolos"?

When checking your list of Unknowns, you may uncover members of the "nolo" clan. If they are among the ones who can't be avoided, let the Decision Maker know of their noncommittal stance ahead of any reference check. This will ensure that the DM sees a "nolo" answer as completely impersonal and will render it of no consequence to your campaign.

Weasels

The Freedom of Information Act and the proliferation of legal eagles have generated a new breed of reference renderers: the group of weasels who intentionally make ambiguous comments. They attempt to protect themselves by making remarks that can be interpreted either pro or con so that nothing can be pinned on them. Here's how they weasel out of committing themselves:

- "Her knowledge of the job was unmatched by those around her."
- "His skill with numbers set him apart."
- "You will be very fortunate if you can get this person to work for you."
- "His word processing skill is amazing considering the experience he has had."
- "In his last job, he was fired with enthusiasm."

These statements are a little like those puzzle drawings that can be interpreted as looking either concave or convex, depending on the bias of the viewer. The words can be interpreted as either positive or negative and serve only to give the weasel something to hide behind.

Don't worry about these types. Any DM worth working for will know what's what and watch with amusement as the weasels wriggle.

Put References to Work

References can work for you if you take the trouble to identify those who support you and program them beforehand with a letter subliminally suggesting the script they should follow. You must also identify the people who are likely to justify their actions at the expense of your career. Discredit them before they can discredit you. Debunk the "nolos" by identifying them to the DM in advance, and ignore the people who can do you no harm.

There's no need to be paranoid about reference checks. There are not that many black hats out there, but, if one should be lying in ambush, you are alert and properly armed. You have no excuse for falling victim to a surprise attack.

Chapter 16

Psychocybernetics and the Job Search

"Wishing may not make it so, but psychocybernetics will definitely help."

It was in the early days of hang gliding, and we had not yet learned to catch the thermals and ride them to higher altitudes. The name of the game was to launch yourself, land, and grab a lift back up, getting in as many flights a day as possible.

One of our favorite places was Pigeon Pass, east of Riverside, California. A 1,000-foot rock outcropping rises from the desert floor. Directly below the takeoff site is one of the larger rocks, about the size of a school bus. It is a cliff launch, with no slope to run down to build up speed—you have to be flying in one step. If you stall on takeoff, the rock beneath becomes your crash site. The wings do not ease your impact, there is no engine to clear a path, and the first thing to hit is the pilot. It's a very personal thing.

"OK, Captain Geritol, you're number one." It was my signal to go. Twenty minutes later, as I was taking down my kite for the next ride up, the other flyers converged on me like ants on a sugar cube, explaining with typical pilot's gestures how I had lifted the nose of my kite as I stepped off the cliff and come very close to a stall and an encounter with the "school bus." They told me that this was a tendency on all my takeoffs. They got my attention.

Psychocybernetics

Thinking about this afterwards, I was reminded of Dr. Maxwell Maltz's book, *Psycho-cybernetics* (Prentice-Hall, Englewood Cliffs, N.J.), in which he describes the closed-loop system in the brain that subconsciously drives us toward the goals we have set. This system operates in much the same way that an airplane on autopilot is directed toward its destination. After the desired heading is cranked in, the autopilot senses any deviations from course and makes the required corrections. If a gust of wind moves the aircraft off the selected course, a signal is sent to the control mechanisms that cancels out this error. The loop is closed, and the aircraft continues on the desired path. This constant error detection and loop closing eventually brings the plane to its destination.

Maltz maintains that we are driven by a similar "servomechanism" (bear with me for a minute with this technical jargon—there's a good point to be made):

> "Cybernetics regards the human brain, nervous system, and muscular system, as a highly complex 'servo-mechanism.' (An automatic goal-seeking machine which 'steers' its way to a target or goal by use of feedback data and stored information, automatically correcting course when necessary.)
>
> "As stated earlier, this new concept does not mean that 'YOU' are a machine, but that your physical brain and body functions as a machine which 'YOU' operate.
>
> "This automatic creative mechanism within you can operate in only one way. It must have a target to shoot at . . . you must first clearly see a thing in your mind before you can do it. When you do see a thing clearly in your mind, your creative 'success mechanism' within you takes over and does the job much better than you could do it by conscious effort, or 'will power.'"

To quote further from Maltz:

> "*Time* magazine reported that when Ben Hogan is playing in a tournament, he mentally rehearses each shot, just before making it. He makes the shot perfectly in his imagination—'feels' the clubhead strike the ball just as it should, 'feels' himself performing the perfect follow-through—and then steps up to the ball, and depends upon what he calls 'muscle memory' to carry out the shot just as he has imagined it.
>
> "Alex Morrison, perhaps the most well-known golf teacher in the world, has actually worked out a system of mental practice. It enables you to improve your golf

score by sitting in an easy chair, and practicing mentally what he calls the 'Seven Morrison Keys.' The
mental side of golf represents 90 per cent of the game,
he says, the physical side 8 per cent, and the mechanical side 2 per cent. In his book, *Better Golf Without
Practice* (New York, Simon and Schuster), Morrison
tells how he taught Lew Lehr to break 90 for the first
time, with no actual practice whatsoever.

"Morrison had Lehr sit in an easy chair in his living
room and relax while he demonstrated for him the
correct swing and gave a brief lecture on the 'Morrison Keys.' Lehr was instructed to engage in no actual
practice on the links, but instead spend five minutes
each day, relaxing in his easy chair, visualizing himself
attending to the 'Keys' correctly.

"Morrison goes on to tell how several days later,
with no physical preparation whatever, Lehr joined
his regular foursome, and amazed them by shooting 9
holes in an even par 36."

Faced with my takeoff problem, I turned to psychocybernetics.
Seated in my living room, I began rehearsing my takeoff run mentally, concentrating on keeping the nose level. I was amazed to
realize that all my takeoffs must have been driven by a subconscious
servomechanism. I was unable to visualize what went through my
mind during the run-up when it is critical that the kite be held in
the right attitude, although I could remember other happenings in
great detail. The programming of my "launch servomechanism"
must have depended on a jumbled accumulation of unanalyzed
inputs from hundreds of flights. Obviously, some defective instructions had crept in to allow the nose to rise to that dangerous angle
of attack.

Sitting in my easy chair, I began to run through the takeoff in my
mind, picturing it from the viewpoint of a disinterested observer. I
looked at the control bar and tried out the position of my hands
necessary to hold the nose at a proper angle for launch. I visualized
how the bar must be moved to maintain this angle while I ran up to
the cliff edge. I pictured the right moment to move my hands into
the flight-control position in anticipation of leaving the hill. Finally, I pictured the kick into the stirrup that initiates prone flight. I
imagined the rush of the wind, the first feeling of lift, and the
sensation of flight. All this was done with the correct nose angle
uppermost in my mind.

According to Dr. Maltz's theory, I was reprogramming my subconscious takeoff servomechanism. I was wiping the old tape and replacing my bad habits with proper launch technique. It worked. I had solved the nose-lifting problem while sitting in my living room. And when I have not flown in several months, I repeat this process from takeoff to landing just to be sure my subconscious servomechanisms are programmed correctly.

Fantasize

So what does all this have to do with getting a better job? You guessed it. Sit in your easy chair and picture yourself in the job you want. Picture the manufacturing line you supervise, the data processing organization, the research lab, the construction site, the aircraft fleet, the office building, your parking space, your associates, your boss, and whatever else comes within the scope of the goal you have targeted. Imagine the start of the day, your drive to work, the meetings and projects and letters and negotiations. . . . Live the job in your mind. Yes, fantasize (always remembering that a fantasy, however good, can never replace real achievement). In your mind, act out how you will relate to the people around you, how your previous experience can be applied, and *how you will make the new boss look good*. Then, when you get to the "end zone," you will act not only as if you've been there but as if you belong there.

John Applies Psychocybernetics

John Allard has targeted Brent, Broderick, & Phillips, a local management consulting firm where his friend Phil works as an accountant. Through Phil, John has learned that the company needs a communications specialist.

Phil gives him some background about the company and its clients, and John does his homework to gather more information about annual sales, number of employees, and principal customers. He reviews the firm's ads in trade magazines to see what it is proud of; he finds out what awards it has won recently. Phil helps his friend further by identifying the Decision Maker, Sheila Atkinson, and provides some insight into her personality. When John picks Phil up for lunch, he is able to get a feel for the place. All of this gives him excellent data to use in planning his approach.

John uses the letters pathway, sending a request for an interview as described in Chapter 3. He follows up by phone and is scheduled for a personal interview with Ms. Atkinson the following Friday at 10 a.m. He has three days in which to fantasize.

One of the definitions of the word "fantasy" is "imagination unrestrained by reality, wild fancy." Another is "an ingenious or highly imaginative creation." John Allard prefers the latter, and, with his favorite chair for transportation, he starts a psychocybernetic voyage as the new communications specialist at Brent, Broderick, & Phillips. His objective is to create a "highly imaginative" program for his subconscious servomechanism to follow as he campaigns for the position. Mentally, John role-plays himself in the position. He visualizes the suits he will wear, the drive to work, the parking lot, and his office. He pictures the people he will be working with. He imagines contacts with clients. He has imaginary conversations with his new boss. John fantasizes original approaches to employee and community relations for the company and lets his imagination roam to include anything that will help him assume the new role. He is giving his subconscious servomechanism a script to follow.

Now he backtracks and rehearses the interview in his mind. He knows he will be asked at least some of the routine interview questions. The first step on his psychocybernetic voyage is to review responses such as these:

> **"I'm selling my business to get out of being on duty seven days a week and to have a more satisfactory family life."**

> **"I consider myself to be a seasoned professional in the communications business. I have the education and the experience. My capability is substantiated by my track record. I believe I can help you reach or exceed your objectives."**

> **"I know that you are looking for a communications specialist to help with your employee relations program. I believe I understand the job, but it would be very helpful to me if you described the important aspects of the position as you see them."**

> **"I do have a resume that I can leave with you."**

> **"I can provide you with excellent references from among my present clients, since they know of my plans. However, I request that you do not contact them until I am being considered seriously for the job."**

This is all routine stuff, and John has practiced it many times before. You have, too, if you've been following the advice of this book. Your having anticipated the questions and practiced your answers will carry you through the interview with ease.

Now John turns to detailed mental role-playing, imagining himself as the employee- and community-communications specialist for BB&P. He bases this on what he has learned about the company. It has 150 employees, bills an estimated $10-million per year, and has after-tax profits in the range of 14 percent. Its stock is sold over the counter. The major stockholder is the founder and CEO, Brian Brophy. The rest of the stock is scattered over a variety of investors. The company provides consulting services, primarily in organizational structure, management information systems, and quality-awareness programs.

The Decision Maker, Sheila Atkinson, is Vice President of Administration, reporting to Brophy. Among other things, she is responsible for the human resources function, including employee and community communications. She is about 45 years old and has been with the company over ten years. Phil thinks she graduated from Vassar. Her salary is guessed to be just under $70K.

The company's ads stress professionalism: "Only the best make the BB&P team." The house organ comes out bimonthly, and, except for what is tacked on the bulletin board, it seems to be the only vehicle by which company information is passed on to the employees. The company is a patron of the Kirby Art Centre, has donated three rooms for the new hospital, maintains a speakers' bureau available to the community, and sponsors Little League and girls' softball teams.

John designs programs in his mind that will make Ms. Atkinson look good. He plans how he would upgrade the company newsletter, publishing it on a monthly basis, incorporating the latest desktop publishing techniques, adding new features like friendly notes from top management, etc. He visualizes plant meetings for all employees that would include specific guest speakers. Among his fantasies is the adoption of an Employee of the Month program.

John imagines how he would amplify the company's community-relations program by adding an Open House day, by increasing United Fund participation, and by implementing a company-sponsored scholarship program. He estimates how much all this is going to cost and formulates a budget. As he continues to program his personal servomechanism, he considers all aspects of the position, *just as if he were in the job.* With the script embedded in his subconscious, John Allard is ready for the interview, way ahead of the candidates who have thought only about what they consider to be the "stress questions" and in another league from those who haven't even gotten that far.

How does he apply all this fantasy to winning the job offer? He weaves the results into the interview, always programmed by his subconscious so that he feels, looks, and acts like the job is his. He asks triggering questions to bring the fruits of his fantasies into reality:

> **"Your bimonthly company newsletter is very professional. I liked the way the employee profile feature was handled. Are there plans to make this a monthly publication?"**

> **"I particularly like your logo. Are you thinking of expanding its use to the company literature?"**

> **"Since the company is growing so rapidly, there is important information that the employees would be very pleased to have on a regular basis. Are there plans to have regular meetings with all the employees?"**

> **"Experience with my clients has proven that the money spent on employee communications is repaid at the bottom line many times over. Do you plan an increase in the budget for this area?"**

John's questions are possible because of the homework he has done gathering information on the company. They are prompts designed to enable him to display the fruits of his psychocybernetic labors: excuses to discuss the specifics of the job that he detailed during his mental role-playing.

When Ms. Atkinson indicates that the publication of the house organ may be stepped up, John can lay out his plan to do just that (exactly as if he were already the communications specialist). He includes his ideas for increased employee participation and the addition of cartoons and occasional friendly notes from the president, always being careful to make it clear that he would not tear down the present effort but build on it.

The question about the logo paves the way for John to lay out his plans to expand its use on letterheads, sales brochures, etc. The question regarding company meetings leads into the presentation of John's ideas for a program of guest speakers, all as he fantasized it in his recliner. Likewise, his budget comments can open the door for a presentation of the budgets he has prepared for the programs designed during his psychocybernetic adventures.

Tread Lightly

Notice that John did not wade into the interview with Ms. Atkinson by saying, "I think your company newspaper needs help. Here is what I am going to do."

Some degree of savoir faire is necessary when playing the role of the incumbent while interviewing for the job. There is a danger of appearing presumptuous and being thrown out as a know-it-all. The role must be well thought out and compatible with the knowledge at hand. The triggering questions must be subtle and the reaction to them evaluated carefully.

If the prompts are sloughed off with very little or no interest, back off. I once set as a target a marketing job with a high-tech company that had announced its plan to sell personal computers. I knew the company would bust its pick if it applied the same sales techniques employed to sell high-tech gear. I had researched the company and thought I had all the information necessary to apply psychocybernetics successfully in preparation for the interview.

Fantasizing in my easy chair resulted in a detailed marketing plan that included definition of the benefits and features that fit the market, as well as designs for sales literature and advertising copy. My triggering question to the vice president of marketing was:

"I think your decision to enter the personal computer market is very timely. Are you going to build your own sales force or start out with reps?"

His response was emphatic. It was as if he had just heard the world's most ridiculous suggestion:

"Oh no! We are going to stick with the same sales force that has made us one of the leaders in minicomputers."

I knew then that this was not the place to present my plans. My research on the company had failed to reveal that the person in charge of marketing was one of those who is convinced high technology sells itself. My fantasies would never get off the ground. Needless to say, the interview did not result in an offer. I'm sure we were both glad.

If Ms. Atkinson bristles when John brings up the company newsletter and it is apparent that she considers it to be just the way she likes it, he had better back off and probe for another opening. Good psychocybernetic work provides other options.

By applying psychocybernetics, John has not merely rehearsed responses to expected questions. He has taken on the image of being in the job. When he appears for the interview, his overall demeanor will state that he belongs in the position. His conduct during the meeting will confirm this impression, because his subconscious servomechanism is driving him toward the target. He looks like he has been there before and acts as if he belongs there.

Where and When

Each of you will have a favorite place where fantasy can flourish. For John Allard, it was his easy chair. Yours may be out on the cabin cruiser or out in the woodshed. I used to favor the shower, but lately I have switched to the bathtub. A recently added bubble machine seems to enhance my ability to imagine as it produces drifts of soapsuds. Try it. It may work for you.

I'm not in the job market, but I am in the process of filling a top management position for a client. In fact, I have already recruited a candidate whom I consider ideal for the job. I am programming my subconscious servomechanism through psychocybernetics so that I will act with assurance to present him in the proper light. This entails fantasizing about my next meeting with the client and about how I will present the recruit's qualifications for the position. This is not unlike preparing for an interview, except for the fee.

Your interviews can affect your whole career. Fantasize! Give your subconscious servomechanisms a vivid target. Apply psychocybernetics to your new-job campaign. Go into your interviews looking and playing the part of the winning candidate. Wishing may not make it so, but psychocybernetics will definitely help.

Chapter 17

Salary and Other Considerations

*"If you can answer 'yes' to these three questions,
you have found a bona fide career path: Is there a job to be
done? Is it a job I can do well? If I do it well, will the right
people know it?"*

Your campaign has been successful so far. The pathways have led you to a Decision Maker. Your telephone discussion earned you an in-person interview. Your resume supported your qualifications for the position, as did your references. You have stressed the positive and avoided negatives and flaws. Rejections along the way have been put in their proper perspective. You have looked and acted as if the job belongs to you and have convinced the DM you will be the best at making him or her look good. You have disclosed your present salary level but have not answered the question of how much money you want. You have said that the important considera-tion for you is career path, and you are confident that a reasonable offer will be made if it is agreed the position is right for you. You have asked for an offer.

You now realize that this is the job you want. The Decision Maker calls you back to the office:

"Congratulations, you have won the job."

You must now cap the success of your job campaign with your handling of the money question. Salary offers can be of three kinds, and there is an appropriate response to each:

- If the offer is ridiculously low, get up and walk out.
- If it is marginal, accept the job and make a date "to work out the details."

- If it is a great offer, accept the job and salary on the spot and go to work that day if you can.

The Very Low Offer

A large company was courting me to accept a vice presidency in international marketing. The interview process was thoroughly mind-boggling. In addition to meeting with the Decision Maker, I was required to perform before the other division presidents, the members of corporate staff, the company shrink, and even some of those who would report to me if I won the job. (This was before I got wise to the fact that you definitely don't want to be interviewed by people who would be working for you.) The DM called me in, graciously announced that I had been selected, and dropped a salary offer on me that was $15,000 below my absolute minimum. Without a microsecond's hesitation, I stood up and moved toward the door, saying,

"Bob, there seems to have been a misunderstanding. If I had realized the value you place on this position, rather than wasting your time and mine, I would have recommended any number of people who are willing to work at that level. There is no way I can accept the job at that salary."

A week later I was called back, and we agreed on a compensation package. I later learned that several managers in the company had been given raises to bring their salaries into line with mine (and with the rest of the industry). None of them even thanked me. I figure it was worth at least a free lunch.

The only effective way to reject a ridiculously low offer is to do so emphatically and on the spot. You will either get a better offer or be sent on your way. There is no sense in pussyfooting around.

The Marginal Offer

Suppose you get an offer for a job that is ideal for you, but the pay is less than you think the job is worth to both you and the company. Your immediate reaction should be:

Say nothing. This is a classic standoff, and the first one who speaks loses. When that marginal offer is made, do anything but speak. Wind your watch, inspect your necktie, rearrange the contents of your purse, stare at the ceiling, or recite the Serenity Prayer mentally: "God grant me the serenity to accept the things I cannot change, the courage to change the things I can, and the wisdom to know the difference." Have the composure not to say anything until the Decision Maker speaks first. Faced with this silent treatment, in a statistically significant number of cases the DM will react by saying something like this:

> "Of course there is some flexibility here, and we could possibly go a bit higher."

Simply by keeping your mouth shut and maintaining a reasonably convincing poker face, you can pick up two or three grand without any hassle. It costs you nothing to try. So here's another rule to write in your hat:

WHEN A MARGINAL SALARY OFFER IS MADE, DON'T SAY A WORD! WAIT FOR THE DM TO SPEAK FIRST.

If this ploy does not work, or if it does, but to a degree that fails to match your reasonable expectations, your next move is to accept the job:

> **"I'm delighted that you have chosen me to join your firm. I accept the job enthusiastically, for I know it is right for both of us. I can't wait to get home and share the news with my husband. I'd like to come back Friday and work out the details."**

You have accepted *the job*. You have not accepted the salary. This is one of the details you will work out when you come back. That date should be at least three days away, so the company will have time to notify the other candidates that the position has been filled. You are then the only one on the scene and in a better negotiating position when you present your case for more money:

> **"My husband and I are very excited about this career opportunity. However, we do not see how we can maintain our standard of living at that salary level. The living costs in this area are much higher than those where we are now. We must cover the cost of moving. My involvement with other companies suggests that similar positions are usually valued more highly in the rest of the industry. We hope you can reconsider your salary offer."**

You then let the chips fall where they may. Having made your play, you may get a better offer. You may settle for the one in hand. The DM may withdraw the original overture. Your urgency factor, the level of the job on the career ladder, and the numbers of people available to fill the position will govern how far you want to carry your demands. If you are at entry level and after a job as a file clerk in a law office, don't dicker. If you are a seasoned administrator with a reputation for getting results, you will have several bidders and can afford to shop yourself around. If you fall somewhere between these two extremes of supply and demand, make a judgment and play your hand. If you've conducted a vigorous campaign, you should have some high cards to play, with a choice of several excellent offers.

Companies like to create the impression that once they have made a salary offer they do not dicker. My experience says that they do. Once they have picked the candidate they want, it is generally better economy for them to increase their offer than get back into the hassle of recruiting and evaluating other candidates.

The Magnificent Officer

When the offer is right, you will know it. Grab it in the same microsecond it would take you to reject a ridiculous offer. There is no better way to join your new company than enthusiastically. Resist any desire to massage your ego by trying to create the impression that you have many choices. At this point, it is far better to appear decisive. Don't say:

> **"Thank you for the offer. I would like a few days to consider it."**

or,

> **"I appreciate the offer but cannot accept at this time because I told another company I would wait to hear from them on Wednesday."**

or,

> **"I want to go home and talk about it with my mother."**

If the job is right and the offer is right, accept with gusto and try to start work the next day. Three months ago, I placed a candidate who received one of these magnificent offers. The job was right.

185

The offer was right. He accepted in the prescribed microsecond and reported to work enthusiastically after giving a respectable two weeks' notice. He called me two months later to announce that he had already earned a raise. His positive mood and manner in accepting the company's proposal immediately and in moving himself into his new career as soon as was practical paid off far beyond either his or my expectations.

Keeping Salary in Perspective

Vince Lombardi is quoted as saying, "Winning isn't everything, it's the only thing." This is great advice for professional football, where it fires up the fierce competitors. On the other hand, the saying "It matters not if you win or lose but only how you play the game" is close to the hearts of those who value sportsmanship and fair play. We amateurs in sports usually find ourselves somewhere between the two.

In the world of business, too, there are those who are in it strictly for the money and those who have pleasure in other aspects of their career. Their biases emerge when it is time to negotiate compensation level. If money is the overriding goal in choosing a career, then play hardball. Get as many offers as you can, play one off against the other, and go with the highest bidder. However, most candidates will opt for a balance between the money and other benefits.

As a recruiter, I am constantly urging candidates to choose the most attractive career path over all other considerations. Experience tells me that the money will follow. My policy is always to recruit candidates on the basis of the career path advantages to them, never compensation level, even though salary is the thing they ask about most frequently. My standard answer is "The job is obviously at a level that would attract you. However, I have no salary specification. If you are the one they want, they will pay a reasonable salary to get you." If I suspect that a candidate is in the job market just to make more money, I will drop him or her from any further consideration. My business depends on a reputation for arranging successful long-term "marriages" in which the best people are placed in long-term careers. I have no interest in the money grabbers; they are job hoppers and will be at it again in two or three years.

I have an acquaintance named Henry who lives in a posh section of Los Angeles and spends his weekends on his million-dollar yacht. He has scrambled for money all his life, walking over anyone in his way. They say, "If you've shaken hands with Henry, be sure to count your fingers." I have another friend who retired in his mid-fifties. He started work as an accountant for a small company and progressed to become its president. He must have managed the operation well, for when the company was acquired his share of the selling price was such that he no longer had to work. He now spends his time traveling and visiting friends, of which he has plenty, me included. Rather than scramble for money, he chose a splendid career path that gave him great satisfaction.

There are many important considerations other than salary, and we are about to look at some of them in detail. Most of them require judgment calls. You won't be able to measure them with a ruler or compute the answers, but careful consideration has got to be better than a blind leap.

You may say you don't have enough information to make judgment calls. If that is the case, you have not worked the problem and are probably waiting for your fairy godmother to set you down in the perfect job. If my lecture on psychocybernetics and fantasizing has encouraged you to believe in magic, I apologize for both Dr. Maltz and myself and suggest that you restudy Chapter 16. Then get back into your psychocybernetic bubble bath and reprogram with a more realistic fantasy.

Career Path and Related Considerations

If you can answer "yes" to these three questions, you have found a bona fide career path: Is there a job to be done? Is it a job I can do well? If I do it well, will the right people know it?

In my entry-level days, I was hired as an engineer by the traveling recruiting team of a large defense contractor. The recruiters convinced me that their programs were of such importance that there was no need for me to meet a Decision Maker or have details of the job I was to do. They told me, "We have so much work to do, you are sure to be assigned to a great job." It did not work out that way. I ended up in an engineering test operation. The two essentials of a challenging career were missing. My work assignments were trivial, and I had no relevant talent to apply to them. Since the company's contract was based on cost plus a fixed fee, I figured I had been hired just to increase billings to the government.

The circumstances were so unfavorable that I quit after three months. On my way out, the company came up with a new assignment that was demanding, needed to be done, and fit my talents. What started out as employment disaster became an important career path. Perhaps it was worth three months of high frustration to learn my lesson and be able to pass this advice along to you: look before you leap, at both the job to be done and your ability to do it.

Don't take anyone's word for anything. Make as careful an evaluation as conditions permit.

The message center in your hat is getting loaded, but here is another dictum worth entering:

IN JOB CHANGING, IT IS NOT SALARY BUT CAREER
PATH CONSIDERATIONS THAT OVERRIDE ALL
OTHER FACTORS.

You will want to have an idea of the relative value of your contribution to the company, your probability for and expected rate of growth, the potential for learning, and the likelihood of compatibility with your peers.

Company Evaluation

You can research the company by asking questions of its management, the Decision Maker, present and past employees, friends, your broker, your reference librarian, and so on. You already will have done a lot of this and will end up with enough information about the company's history, size, reputation, ownership, and management to grade it on the factors that are important to you. Do you understand the management's growth philosophy and operating style? How close to retirement are individual managers? Ask the DM direct questions about the potential for growth in the position. No need to be bashful. The last thing the company wants is to hire someone who doesn't care.

Compatibility with the Decision Maker

This is the toughest judgment to make in advance. Newlyweds are warned that the most important decision they will make is choosing a house, but that is considerably easier than choosing a boss. You can measure a house with a tape measure, and you know that the house you choose will be there next year.

Have dinner with your prospective DM. Stay alert and you can learn a lot from the little things. What does the DM like to eat? How much does the DM like to eat? What subjects are chosen for idle chatter? What can you tell about the DM's social graces and temperament, particularly in relation to the employees of the restaurant? Do you feel there is any empathy between you? Do you have any interests in common? Are there any inklings of an ability to teach or a willingness to share?

When you choose a house, you know that it will be yours as long as you keep up the payments. This is not true of bosses, who often move on to other pursuits. There is nothing you can do about it. There is one similarity, however, between buying a house and starting a new job. You can't choose your neighbors, and you can't choose your coworkers either. Good luck with both.

Location

Location considerations are very personal. If you will take any job as long as it means you can stay in your present house, your decision is easy. If the new situation requires a 90-minute commute on the L.A. freeways twice a day, then for me the answer would also be easy, not just "no" but "hell, no." If accepting the new job would require packing up and moving 1,500 miles to Cleveland, you had better find out whether this fits in with your spouse's plans. If you have a daughter or son in high school, moving the family becomes a major decision. You will be leaving friends and possibly relatives behind. Can you make new friends easily?

Be particularly careful to evaluate cost-of-living differentials. If you are moving from Lansing, Michigan, to Los Angeles, California, be prepared for a surprise. A substantial salary increase may seem attractive, but only if the additional income is not eaten up by the cost of rent or real estate, food, clothing, etc. At this writing, the same $107,000 house in Lansing would cost $320,000 in a Los Angeles suburb. And then there's the climate to consider.

Relocation Costs

Take a close look at the expense of moving. Company policies concerning the relocation costs of new employees range from "get there on your own" to coverage that includes as many trips as it takes you to find a new home and living expenses at the new location during the transition period, the transportation of household goods, the costs of selling your old home and buying your new one, a lump-sum payment to cover incidentals, and in some cases even the purchase of your old home from you if you cannot sell.

You have accepted the job or both job and salary. In either case, there are still some details to be worked out, among them relocation expenses. Even though personnel directors will try and convince you that policy is policy and there are no exceptions, moving allowances *are* negotiable. The company can adjust its standard policy, depending on its degree of interest in you, which is to some extent a function of supply and demand. If you new job had been filled from inside the company by an employee who had to relocate, the employer would probably have covered all the costs mentioned above. So there is some latitude on this issue if you are valuable enough to the company. Play your hand, but not beyond the value of the cards you actually hold.

Be absolutely sure that there is mutual agreement as to exactly which expenses will and will not be covered. You should have it in writing, not because you don't trust the DM or the company but only because nobody would know of your agreement if the DM were suddenly run over by a trolley car. So take this precaution for your own peace of mind, or, when the dust of moving clears, you may find that you're making mortgage payments on two houses at once and what was supposed to be a brave new start has become an ordeal. I've been there and I know.

Perquisites

"Perks" are benefits over and above salary and the costs of getting you on board. They range from the basics offered by most companies to the splendid enhancements provided to particularly highly valued employees.

The basics include paid vacation time, maternity leave, and health insurance, as well as credit union membership, employee savings and stock plans, performance incentives, and, for outside salespeople, use of a company car. Depending on the company, some of the other perks may include bonuses, stock options, profit sharing, extended vacations (perhaps at the company retreat), a private secretary and office, a personal parking space, a chauffeured limousine, a seat on the corporate jet, country club membership, maybe even a cabin cruiser.

Again, you have to evaluate your position on the supply-and-demand curve and play your cards accordingly. However, remember that a good negotiator never makes a *final* final offer. Always leave yourself a place to go when it becomes apparent you have pushed too far:

"In thinking it over, my position on the cabin cruiser does seem a bit unrealistic. How about a ten-speed bike instead?"

Give the company an easy way to back off from its cutoff point. Do it neatly and with good grace. You got them to go as far as they would (or could), but they won the last point.

Employment Contracts

I have not had an employment contract since leaving Uncle Sam's Air Force, so the following will be laced with some theory. There are contracts that place requirements on the employee and others that place requirements on the employer. The first type usually stipulates:

- That all inventions and patents belong to the company.
- That the employee will safeguard all company secrets.
- That the employee agrees not to leave and work for a competitor for a specified period, often one or two years.

There is sometimes a supplement to this "noncompetition clause" that states: "If the employee is unable to obtain employment consistent with his or her abilities and education because of the limitations imposed by the agreement not to compete, then the company shall bind him or her to the agreement only as long as the company pays 50 percent of the employee's salary prior to leaving the company or makes up the difference between what the employee used to make and can earn when complying with the agreement."

Some companies enforce these provisions with vigor. Others let them slide. My experience suggests that such contracts are difficult to defend in most courts, though some of the larger companies have been able to use them very effectively.

The second type of contract, which places requirements on the employer, is offered to certain high-level managers and valuable specialists. These contracts guarantee employment for a stated number of years and at a specified minimum salary. Firms use the security provided by such contracts to attract top candidates to new situations that may involve great responsibility, difficult tasks, high risks, or some combination of the three. Arrangements of this sort are usually necessary to entice a recognized leader or expert away from a position that is both rewarding and satisfying.

These contracts work. Three years ago, an acquaintance of mine took a job as president of a company that was in such a bad way there was doubt that anything could save it. He was widely recognized as a leader in his industry and had been expected to move up to the presidency of his old company within the year. When asked why he had made such a sudden and unpromising change, he answered, "They made me an offer I couldn't refuse." You can bet he sits behind his new desk protected by a very healthy employment contract.

Chapter 18

For Entry-Level Candidates

"Nobody lacks experience. Stop using that excuse for not finding an entry-level job."

Last year I recruited a young woman who had a master's degree in mechanical engineering from Rensselaer Polytechnic Institute, where she had studied with one of the top people in the field. She was working in the catalog order department of Sears. When I flew back from Washington, D.C., a couple of months ago, my seatmate turned out to be another young engineer who had graduated recently from a major southern university. He had found a job working as a photographer.

At a trade show last month, I met and talked to several young people who were or were soon to be "freshouts"—fresh out of college—and was astonished to hear of the difficulties they were encountering in entering the job market. Last week, I attended a high school graduation party for a neighbor's daughter and there chatted with her and her friends about their plans for the future. Those who weren't going to college seemed to have the attitude that they were not going to have much choice and would take any job they could get.

The catalog clerk and photographer were underemployed. The freshouts were discouraged, and the high school grads seemed to be floundering. None of them seemed to know how to improve their career potential. This made me realize that my book would be incomplete without an examination of the special circumstances of people entering the job market for the first time. Although special problems do exist, they can be handled, just like all the other problems we have come up against. However, it is up to the freshouts themselves to supply the solutions.

Placement Programs

Generally, freshouts at both the high school and college level indicate that institutional placement programs did not provide as much help as they had expected or hoped for. The ones who feel otherwise have usually augmented the system with steps of their own. Getting good grades is a great start, and there are other important steps we will cover.

The Career Planning and Placement Service at the University of New Hampshire is a good example of the kind of help colleges can provide their students. Its services include tips on correspondence, resume guidelines, hints on interview etiquette, an information interviewing program, and guidance concerning second interviews. The information interview program is particularly good. It consists of a network of over 1,000 alumni and parents who have volunteered to serve as contacts in their fields. Students can meet with contacts and learn about career prospects in the fields that interest them. Incidentally, they gain experience in talking with professionals in a business setting. Although the "interviews" are not job-hunting expeditions, at the very minimum they probably provide some excellent leads along with the useful information.

Some colleges offer courses on how to find a job for credit. Others run career planning seminars for juniors and seniors. But the bedrock of most colleges' job-placement programs is the on-campus interview conducted by a company's recruiting team. These interviews are arranged in a variety of ways. At San Jose State, for example, the program is computer based. A brochure is circulated that announces the schedule of visiting companies and describes the job openings at each. Interested students apply for up to ten interviews by completing a registration form on which they describe their background and experience. The students are then matched with companies' needs and scheduled for interviews. The recruiting teams' openings are usually easily filled, especially the more attractive ones. If there are still job slots left open after the computer matching, there is a manual sign-up system. The strength of this system is that it sidesteps "political" and personal considerations; however, it is possible for a student to go through the entire procedure and not get a single desirable interview.

Cooperative Programs

At the high school level, job-placement efforts seem to rely on job banks and cooperative programs, with emphasis on the latter. In a job bank, companies call or mail in their job requirements, and counselors match the openings with suitable students. Here in

Florida, at least, high schools don't wait for this process to bring in the jobs. Through active cooperative programs, members of the counseling staff work with local business and industry to find or even create jobs for students. Cooperative programs enable students to gain work experience, job skills, and a practical understanding of potential career paths while they are still in school.

Cooperation with industry and business is a major facet of college job-placement programs also. Students who want to evaluate potential career paths, begin their transition from the academic world, establish valuable professional contacts, and, if the assignment fits, obtain an early career start are well served by these programs. The cooperative system also provides an important resource for recruiters. Companies that have no full-time vacancies are often glad to give recruiters the names of people who have worked for them part-time while in college. I have recruited outstanding candidates in this way, since the students who do take advantage of cooperative programs are often high academic achievers also.

No Placement Automats

Never think of high school or college placement services as automatic career machines. You can't walk up, plug in your resume, and come away with the ideal job. You have to work the system and sometimes work around the system. If the freshout's most common complaint is that companies only hire experienced people, another is that the big companies visit the big colleges and hire the high averages, leaving everyone else on their own. I'm convinced that this is an accurate appraisal of the situation for students with less than the best grades, whether in high school or college. My message for them is to stop looking around for someone to help them and do something to help themselves. And what can they do to help themselves? Apply all the techniques and tactics described in this book. Use all the tools and travel all the pathways.

Commencement is no time to begin wondering what you're going to do. You should have at least a broad objective when you graduate from high school. If you are not going to college, have something more specific in mind than just "to get a job." If you do go to college, your career planning should start in your freshman year and continue right through graduation. Work part-time while in high school or college, take summer jobs, take advantage of information interviews, get into a cooperative program. This will certainly help your economic situation, but, more importantly, it will help you evaluate potential career paths. If none of these options is available through the official channels, create them for yourself. I've heard of high school students who volunteered to work for nothing in order to gain experience they particularly wanted.

The way to separate yourself from the herd is by working the problem more vigorously than the rest. Don't sit around hoping for some smooth-running machine to drive you effortlessly to the cushy career of your lifetime. Start early to evaluate, plan, and implement, so that when your day arrives to switch the tassel you will be ready to enter your career rather than just starting to think about it.

When you get in the job cafeteria line for the first time, you don't want to just grab the first entree you see. You want to have a choice of your first job, and you certainly don't want to be stuck taking the only one you can get. Either way, your first job may not be a good fit. In fact, the odds of your striking it right in your first job are very small. Like most of us, you will probably slip into something indirectly or make several changes before you feel comfortable with your career, and that's OK. Don't be disappointed if your first choice does not work out. But this is not to minimize the importance of having that choice. It is a knack that will stand you in good stead throughout your working life.

Disillusioned Butterflies, Determined Butterflies

As we've said, the most commonly heard complaint from people new to the job fray is "Companies only hire people with experience. How can I gain experience if I can't get a job?" I call this the "disillusioned butterfly syndrome": "Here I am, a beautiful butterfly. Who cares? Everyone wants experience, and all I've done is caterpillar." The resume of a disillusioned butterfly would read something like this:

Delbert Butterfly
South Meadow

Objective: To join a group in a field where nectar is abundant and the winds gentle.

Qualifications: Metamorphosed yesterday in Farmer Brown's barn.

Prior Experience: Four weeks as a caterpillar in Farmer Brown's garden.

A determined butterfly, on the other hand, takes a positive approach and would write a profile along these lines:

Rex Butterfly
South Meadow

Objective: To enter a field where I will have the opportunity to provide beauty and to pollinate.

Qualifications: Metamorphosed yesterday in Farmer Brown's barn.

Prior Experience: Four weeks as a caterpillar in Farmer Brown's garden, where I stripped three azalea bushes, gobbled a hibiscus, surprised Farmer Brown's children, and grew healthy and ready for change.

Mother Nature's Choice

Mother Nature has an important opening for a butterfly at the botanical gardens. Which one will she hire? Right again, but don't forget to give some credit to your coach. Naturally, Nature is going to pick the determined butterfly—its resume conveys understanding of caterpillar responsibilities and provides testimony that they were carried out appropriately. A diligent caterpillar will most likely perform well as a butterfly. The disillusioned butterfly may do just as well, but, when she's offered the choice, why should Nature take chances?

Escape the Net

In Chapter 4, I mentioned that the lack of a list of accomplishments was a major deficiency in many of the resumes I receive each week. The seasoned campaigner who provides this information has a substantial advantage over those who do not. For you freshouts, this takes on even greater importance. Of course, entry-level candidates have no previous positions to refer to or are limited to part-time or cooperative education experiences, so you will have to dig into your past for successes you can describe. Tout them. It is the most important step in putting yourself ahead of the entry-level herd and earning the first job of your choice. Nobody lacks experience. Stop using that excuse for not finding an entry-level job.

Michelle Is Determined

Michelle Robbins is the daughter of a very good friend. She had chosen not to go to college, and life was jostling her around as she worked at a series of typical teenage jobs: hostess, boutique clerk, waitress, receptionist. She felt there must be more satisfying career paths, but since she "had no experience" she believed they were not for her.

Michelle was bobbing along in the stream until her mother and I got together with her and we three began to examine her situation. This resulted in some new one-page resumes and a job-search plan that earned her five interviews and three fine offers in the first two weeks of her campaign. Instead of presenting herself as a disillusioned butterfly, Michelle applied what I taught her. She began by accepting a position as an administrative clerk and has moved up to manage marketing for a high-tech computer company.

This is how it worked. Michelle decided that office administration would be a productive career path for her and wrote a resume substantiating her qualifications and supporting her campaign. She used the essentials of this profile in the presentations she made by letter, cold-calling, and answering ads. A copy of her resume appears on the following page.

Let's evaluate this resume against the resume rules. Michelle has targeted office administration and says so in her statement of objective. She kept her resume to one page. Her company-oriented statement of objective is clear and to the point. (Compare the statements of Delbert and Rex Butterfly and you will see how Rex's words gave Mother Nature more reason to choose him. Michelle's words do the same in stating that she would like to contribute to the company's success.)

Michelle includes accomplishments by mentioning how she helped create a good office atmosphere, attended to the needs of diners, was promoted to supervisor, and won the highest award for gymkhana. She does not state salary requirements, and she establishes her age bracket sufficiently by saying that she is seeking an entry-level position.

Michelle put her high school education at the end, which is where it should be in her case. Job hopping does not apply to Michelle. She includes no superfluous information: no health statements; no references; no clubs, religious affiliations, political preferences, etc.

The key to the success of this resume is Michelle's compliance with the rule concerning accomplishments. Instead of skulking into the job market as an apologetic novice with no experience, Michelle let the business world know that she had both experience *and* accomplishments. No disillusioned butterfly anymore, she told everyone that she had a performance record to be proud of. She presented herself as a valuable business resource rather than

RESUME

Michelle Robbins
3396 Benjamin Court
Hartford, CT 06107
203-555-0131

OBJECTIVE
To secure an entry-level position in office administration where I can contribute to the success of the company and at the same time learn additional career skills.

WORK EXPERIENCE
June 1986–August 1987: Receptionist/General Office Worker, Professional Estimates, Inc., Hartford

Responsibilities included reception, answering the telephone, and doing some filing and light typing. Contributed to an efficient and friendly office environment.

October 1984–August 1987: Waitress/Hostess, Captain Ed's Crab House and The Sanctuary, West Hartford

As a hostess, was responsible for greeting and seating the guests and ensuring that they felt welcome and comfortable. As a waitress, was cheerfully attentive and promptly satisfied the needs of my customers.

September 1983–October 1984: Salesperson/Supervisor, M. Mason & Company, Hartford

As a salesperson, helped customers in the women's sportswear department. After five months, was promoted to supervisor, responsible for check approval, money management, and the handling of customer complaints.

EDUCATION
High school graduate, West Hartford High School, 1982

AWARDS/SPECIAL INTERESTS
Highest Achievement Award for gymkhana (horsemanship); additional firsts, seconds, and thirds throughout the years. Also enjoy bicycle riding and taking care of animals.

merely a decorative but inexperienced butterfly. Her gymkhana awards supported her case, showing that she had been active and achievement oriented in her caterpillar years.

Ken Works the Problem

At the aforementioned trade show, I shared a lunch table with a young man named Ken and soon realized that I was in the presence of an exceptional person. He was about to graduate from an excellent college with a mechanical engineering degree and a grade point average (GPA) of 3.5. He could have ridden his GPA to a top job with one of the biggies that visited his campus. In fact, he already had an offer from the company he had worked for under the college's cooperative program. Nonetheless, he was attending the convention at his own expense as part of his job-finding campaign. Sitting around waiting for something to happen was not for Ken, nor was taking the first thing that came along.

Our conversation soon centered on job search in general and Ken's efforts in particular. He showed me his resume. On a scale of 10, his was a 9. (We experts never admit to finding perfection in our field. There is always room for improvement.) His statement of objective was clear and was not egocentric. Its one weakness, if it had one, was that it was not company oriented.

"OBJECTIVE: Materials Engineer seeking a position in the composite materials industry."

The resume sparkled with accomplishments:

- Earned a 3.5 GPA.
- Aided in the design of new bicycle components utilizing advanced composites.
- Codeveloped manufacturing processes for composite bicycle components.
- Advised on all sales aspects of these new components.
- Created, coached, captained, secured sponsorships for, and managed the financial affairs of three competitive cycling teams with great success.

Ken was not at the convention simply to pass out resumes, nor did he frequent the employment booth where I had interviewed other freshouts. He was working the show: collecting literature, meeting the participants and taking their business cards, learning the products, getting himself known. He was there for the full three days, and I believe he worked harder than I did (and I was earning my living!). I have recommended that you aim for three good offers, but a guy like this could end up with twenty.

It's up to You

So you don't have a 3.5 GPA. The marks didn't come easy to you, or maybe you took the toughest course offered while supporting a family. No need to file this book away with your diploma and year-book and pretend to be contented with underemployment. Michelle was no great student, yet she is one of the brightest and most determined people I know. If she had been content with what her GPA predicted, she would still be at the restaurant, cussing out the kind of people who don't leave tips. Instead she is on a great career path.

If you know the biggies are not going to pick you when they descend on your campus, pick *them* instead. Execute a letter cam-paign like the one described in Chapter 3. Sell your accomplish-ments so strongly that the Decision Maker instructs the recruiting team to seek you out as soon as they hit town. Or better still, bypass the on-campus system entirely and win an invitation to be inter-viewed on your own.

I wrote this chapter so that the special circumstances of you entry-level candidates could be covered, but don't infer that the rest of the book isn't for you. The tools, pathways, and techniques are just as relevant to you as to those who have already entered the business or industry orbit.

There is no such thing as a free lunch at any level, so work the problem and reap the rewards . . . three good offers or maybe twenty. There's no automatic career machine either, so don't be content to let "the system" lead you to your career path. Sure, use the system for all it's worth, but make that extra effort to get ahead of the pack. Keep in mind that winning by an inch earns the prize just as well as winning by a mile.

Don't be intimidated by the higher GPAs or the degrees from better-known schools. Don't worry about the degree you don't have. Tout yourself. Lay on the accomplishments. Sell yourself as a complete package and you can win with inches to spare.

Hello, Young Workers

It has been a pleasure talking to you and thinking about your special circumstances. Perhaps it's from being the father of nine or from hang gliding with much younger people for the past fifteen years, but I have great faith in you. You just may be able to straighten out the mess that my generation is leaving you. Before *I* leave you, I can't resist taking the opportunity to hand out some more advice. (It's my book, and I can if I want.)

I have told you and told you that the key to getting three good offers is to work the problem. I've told you not to depend on the system to do the job for you and to stop looking around for help that's not there. Now comes the switch, my version of "stop and smell the flowers."

When I was 18, the Army Air Corps put me through Aviation Cadet Training. I had an airplane to fly around in and do all kinds of wildly exciting things with: loops, stalls, flying under bridges. It was a young man's dream come true, but as I look back I realize that I was so intent on not washing out of the program that I was hardly able to savor the great adventure of it while it was happening.

One incident that occurred during the flight training will show you what I mean. The instructors always called us "Kaaadets," which was no title of respect. In fact, I would say it conveyed a thinly veiled hatred based on a thinly veiled mortal fear. Because their lot in life was to sit in the back seat of a B-13 basic trainer and try to keep the Kaaadet up front from killing them.

One day, our instructor bellowed at me and a buddy, "Kaaadets, grab your chutes. We're going to do some formation flying." Now this instructor was either very brave or very crazy. Not only did he want to fly in formation, but he wanted to fly in *close* formation with a couple of student pilots who could hardly find the pilot relief tube. My plane was to the left of his, and he was not satisfied until my right wingtip trailed his left one by no more than 3 feet and overlapped it by at least a foot. I concentrated my gaze on two rivets in his wing and kept them in the same relative position no matter what gyrations he put his plane through. He gave us all sorts of hand signals: "Increase RPM." "Fuel to rich." "Open canopy." "Drop three-quarter flaps." And then we touched the ground!

This character had brought us back to the field and landed us in close formation, but I had been so busy concentrating on those rivets that I had had no idea of what was happening. I was one surprised Kaaadet when I felt the earth under my wheels. I had missed the exhilaration of making my first formation landing.

My message is simple. Enjoy what you are doing. Enjoy it now, right now. Don't wait until you're remembering it tomorrow to appreciate today. Savor the adventure while it is happening. Enjoy it now, grow now, learn now and not in retrospect.

Chapter 19

For Mature Candidates

"Age discrimination is real, but there is plenty you can do to fight it."

The fastest-growing segment of our society is composed of people over 60, growing older and wiser and unable to do a single thing about it. Happily, all of the job-finding techniques we have discussed so far apply to the mature worker. In Chapter 4 we looked at ways of handling the age question on resumes, and in Chapter 6 we considered the relationship between age and the relative importance of the different pathways. Because some employers seem to think that getting older means getting less useful, this chapter will look in detail at other considerations that apply specifically to mature candidates.

Although the "age problem" must be acknowledged, the good news is that it can be handled. Age discrimination is real, but there is plenty you can do to fight it. For one thing, the years are operating in our favor. There is a developing shortage of qualified workers that will change attitudes toward mature candidates in a hurry. More immediately, an increasing number of enlightened managers are realizing that there is a source of valuable experience in senior citizens and their near kin. Look no further than the incredible turnaround of Chrysler by Lee Iacocca, whose team of eight key players included three former Ford employees whom he brought out of retirement. With our years actually working *for* us and more managers seeing the signal flare sent up by Iacocca, mature candidates are going to fare increasingly well in the employment market. I predict fewer early and forced retirements and more hiring of retirees.

Only Temporary?

One of the unspoken considerations in the decision not to hire an older person is that the company wants someone who can be expected to stay around for a long time. A 60-year-old new hire would be expected to retire at 65, and companies shy away from hiring someone on so "temporary" a basis. This is high-intensity bureaucratic smog. Look around you. How many people do you know who have stayed in the same company for five years? Not many, I'll bet, given the fluidity of the current employment scene. This is a very poor excuse for not hiring a mature candidate.

Whenever I deal with a company that I sense is reluctant to consider an older candidate, I propose a scheme to offset the "only temporary" objection. I recommend that they hire my candidate with the stipulation that the person retire at the end of a specified period (say five years) and leave behind a qualified replacement. And if the replacement has been trained to a specified level of proficiency, the retiree is awarded a $10,000 honorarium. This seems like a win-win situation to me, but I have to admit I haven't been able to sell the concept, though I'll continue to try.

Older Is Better

Studies of older workers have brought to light some interesting data. The American Association of Retired Persons reports that productivity does not decline with age, and that workers 45 years and older have attendance records equal to or better than those of workers in most other age groups. Insurance company statistics reveal that people 55 and over make up 13.6 percent of the work force but account for only 9.7 percent of those injured in the workplace. People 45 years and older take no more sick days than younger employees do. Employees between the ages of 50 and 60 have been employed by their companies for an average of fifteen years, much longer than younger members of the work force.

One of the arguments against hiring older workers is that it runs up insurance costs, but the accident and sick-day data dispute this. A study that compared the health-care costs of older and younger workers based on data from Blue Cross–Blue Shield's Federal Employee Program, the nation's largest group health insurance plan, revealed that the differences were not great enough to warrant such costs being a factor in employment decisions. The excuse of higher insurance costs is discredited.

Combine these data with the other advantages that older workers bring with them and they become such bargains you wonder how employers can afford not to hire them. I realize, of course, that I'm preaching to the converted in this particular church, and much missionary work remains to be done to win management over to our cause.

Consider This

A company decided to enter a new market with a new product. This required the installation and shakedown of new and complicated equipment. The company had the choice of hiring one of the top three experts in the field, all of them older. In spite of very strong advice against it from a consultant specializing in the industry and its technology, the firm hired a youngster who had a mere three years' experience with similar equipment.

Tons of scrap and three years later, the company hired the best of the three who had been available earlier. He was pushing 60, did not have a degree, and probably reported to the new job without having shined his shoes, but he was clearly the complete expert. Three months later, he got his first raise. What he did was only what he could have done three years earlier . . . at a saving of an estimated $1-million in scrap and wasted effort.

Join Forty-Plus and Ply the Pathways

The older candidate's first move should be to join Forty-Plus or a similar program. This will give you a valuable operating base, with all the tools you need to pursue the pathways.

All that has been said so far about the pathways applies to the older worker, with a slight shift of emphasis. To reiterate, the friends and associates pathways are always of primary importance, except perhaps in the case of entry-level candidates, but for mature workers they are especially significant and come close to being the only way into a job. As the age of candidates increases, so does the percentage of those who find their new job or career through a friend or acquaintance, until I would estimate that it reaches 90 percent for those hired at the age of 65 or over.

Faced with this data, you know what to do. This is not to imply that the other pathways won't help you, but do use your judgment in allocating your efforts. The former vice president of operations of a Fortune 500 company should not go from company to company filling out employment applications. He's bound to scare some people into thinking their jobs are at risk. Nor should a purchasing manager coaxed into early retirement spend much time with recruiters, who, whether they admit it or not, will be looking for youngsters.

Other Options

There are other ways that can be particularly attractive to the mature worker. You can start a business, buy a business, or become a consultant. You can "renew," entering a new field in which your experience and maturity are applicable. You can take a "keep-busy" job, or you can putter at your hobby (whittling, fly tying, rose growing, writing, sewing, etc.) and call it a business.

Start a Business

Obviously you will want to pick a product or service where you can apply your experience. Carefully forecast sales and expenses. Two weeks later, redo your forecast. Wait one more week and then:

- Cut your sales forecast in half.
- Double your "guesstimate" of expenses.
- Only then do a cash-flow analysis for the first three years. This is simply a calculation of the business checkbook balance for each of the next thirty-six months.
- Finally, anticipate the miracles it will take to cover your expenses during start-up.

All this is simply another way of advising you to make conservative forecasts and be sure you have enough capital. New businesses fail not because of poor management, inadequate products, or the lack of a market. They fail because they run out of money before their balloon gets off the ground.

Buy a Business

Success in buying yourself a job by acquiring a business depends on matching your finances, talents, and interests with the enterprise. Rules to remember:

- If an audit does not confirm the after-tax income you need, don't take a chance.
- Don't pay anything for "goodwill" that will walk out the door with the previous owner.
- Be absolutely sure that you will have enough cash to weather the transition period.
- To the extent possible, finance the purchase out of future operating profits. There is no better way to measure viability than to keep the previous owner on the hook for payments out of profits.

Become a Consultant

This is a special case of starting a business. People who have gone into consulting will tell you it's not a bad business . . . until you run out of friends. The renowned experts with a waiting list of eager clients are the exceptions.

One great way to get started is to consult with the outfit you have just left. This gives you time to develop a broader base. It will take some hard work, but once you are established, you will find consulting fun and rewarding, if occasionally frustrating when clients don't take your astute advice.

Renew

"Renew" is a buzzword I have picked up from recent "maturity" literature: "Don't retire, renew." The January 1989 issue of *New Choices* (Retirement Living Publishing, New York) tells of five people, ranging in age from their mid-fifties to late sixties, who chose not to retire but to enter new fields. They were:

- The ex-president of a large corporation who opened a pizza parlor.
- A teacher who entered government service.
- A former dentist who became a consulting anthropologist.
- A onetime social worker who became a stand-up comedian.
- An appliance dealer who went back to college and became a lawyer.

I see great opportunities for mature workers to renew their careers in what I call Prado's-Law positions (Prado's Law: 20 percent of the people produce 80 percent of the results). These include jobs in real estate, insurance, telemarketing, recruiting, and the like, jobs that depend on self-motivation and individual effort. These are usually not salaried positions, so compensation is directly proportionate to results. Many mature workers have the combination of experience, energy, and judgment that enables them to perform in the 20-percent group and establish viable new careers.

Keeping Busy

If income is not an issue, there are abundant activities that will keep you from getting bored, from volunteer work at the local hospital to service in the Peace Corps. (There is no age limit for Peace Corps volunteers. Assignments are usually for two years. Living expenses are covered, and $200 per month is held in escrow to be paid at the end of the tour.)

Our government has been relaxing regulations covering certain kinds of work in the home. It is now legal for companies to hire homeworkers to make gloves and mittens, and it is expected that such items as buttons, buckles, handkerchiefs, and jewelry will be added to the list. This sort of thing could be good "keep-busy" work for those who aren't content to be couch potatoes.

The Hobby Shop

Another way to go is to turn your hobby into a business. This may look like a good way of writing off some costs as business expenses, but Big Brother will be watching. If you don't turn a profit soon enough to satisfy the IRS, you may be billed for back taxes. See your accountant.

Don't Be Greedy

If you were with your last employer long enough to become vested, you are assured of a pension payment each month. In shopping for a new job, do not insist that you get paid as much as or more than you received in your last position. Your old salary plus your pension could be more than you have ever made. By insisting on receiving your previous level of compensation, you might miss out on an attractive new career slot at a moderate salary that, when combined with your pension, would maintain you at your accustomed standard of living.

Attitude

Having advised the freshouts to enjoy the adventure while it's happening, I feel it's only fair to leave you mature candidates with words of at least equal profundity. (Remember, it's still my book.) Here comes another story, along with my version of the power of positive thinking, which I prefer to call "attitude control."

I was on a scuba expedition to the Cortez Bank, some 30 miles off the coast of San Diego. The voyage had to be made at night so the skipper could home in on the single lighted buoy. The dive had to be made at absolute high tide, since a rising tide would wash us back to San Diego and a falling tide would send us to Hawaii. The prize for all this trouble was black coral.

At the time I had two cracked ribs, earned in a magnificent dive off a 6-foot ladder to save a $3.65 can of paint. I started my dive at dawn and soon found myself at a depth of about 35 feet hanging on to a large banana kelp with both hands as the surge swept me 12 feet one way and then 12 feet the other. There were 4-foot swells at the surface, which meant an 8-foot differential between the peaks and troughs, and I could feel the pressure changes in my ears. This was definitely a big guy's dive, and I was soon convinced I was over my head in more ways than one and started back to the boat. As I broke the surface, terror struck. There was no boat! They had sailed off and left me in the middle of the ocean! Then I rose on a swell, as did the boat. As I clambered aboard, the pain from my ribs was excruciating, but I was saved.

Later that morning, I noticed an old-timer who I figured must be the deckhand. He looked around 70 years old, and what little hair he had was close-cropped. Something about him made me think "ex-Marine," though he was slight of build and by no means a "macho man." And then he started putting on a wet suit that looked as if it had met with a strain of moths that devoured rubber. I was wondering whether he'd even be able to lift his tank.

While I was entertaining these thoughts, the old-timer threw his tank over his head and onto his back, strapped on his lead, spit-cleaned and adjusted his mask, and did a back dive into the Pacific. The next time we saw him, he was returning with an empty tank and a beautiful fan of black coral, the only specimen brought on board during that trip.

On the long ride back, we learned that he was in fact 75. As far as he was concerned, diving at his age was no big deal. His attitude was so positive that the difficulty and quality of the dive he had just completed probably never even occurred to him. He was a shining example of maturity crowned by a positive attitude.

If you are an environmentalist and are concerned that the Cortez Bank was being raped of her black coral, rest easy. Mother Nature has given the bank great built-in protection, and I'm sure she doesn't begrudge having given up a prize to the old-timer.

So you mature candidates need not relegate yourselves to the ranks of the couch potatoes. Remember Dr. Maltz's psychocybernetics, Johnny Mercer's accent on the positive, Roger Miller's roller skates, and the scuba-diving old-timer. Fantasize about what you want to be and where you want to go. Use the tools and pathways. Maybe you won't dive the Cortez Bank at age 75, but then again you might . . . while on holiday from your new career.

Chapter 20

Success at Your
New Job

*"Taking over in your new job should be an infiltration rather
than a frontal attack."*

If you expect this to be a rehash of material from the American
Management Association, the Harvard Business School, and Peter
Drucker, then you're going to be disappointed. Instead of management theory, you are going to get practical rules for success in a new
job that have been forged and tempered in the furnace of organizational encounters.

Play the Power Structure

General Electric's Professional Business Management Course
taught me POIM (Plan, Organize, Integrate, and Measure). A good
manager or worker plans the work to be done, organizes it into a
practical arrangement, integrates this organization within itself
and the larger whole, and sets up systems to measure the results
against the plan. Whether your new job requires you to take over a
public relations department, an automatic production line, or anything else, the first thing you should do is be sure the work has been
planned, organized, and integrated, and that measures have been
established so you can dig in and get the job done. Right? Wrong!

THE FIRST THING FOR YOU TO DO IS TO FIGURE
OUT THE POWER STRUCTURE.

The public relations department and production line and everything else were running before you got there and will most likely

continue running while you attend to first things first. Find out where the power lies so you can set up your plan for success, which is in essence a plan for survival.

Consider the career of an elected official who is sincerely dedicated to establishing good government. In order to accomplish this mission over the long haul, the politician has to survive reelection after reelection. You were "elected" when you convinced the Decision Maker you were the one to make him or her look good. If you are going to reach your goals at the new company, you must continue to be "reelected," keeping the DM and all the others in the power structure reassured that you will continue to be the one to make them all look good. Setting up a plan to ensure your survival is your first priority.

Hal Springfield was a real pro. I had just moved in from another company and had become his boss. On the second day that I was in my new office he showed up, having traveled from his office, which was 750 miles away. He was wasting no time in getting a reading on this new element in his power structure. Over the years, he proved to be as good as they come in reading the lines of power: not the most capable and a little lazy, he always had me convinced that he supported my goals and wanted to make me look good. Bill Post was a better manager, but I never really felt I had his full backing. Hal got the next promotion. Be a Hal and not a Bill.

Know the Players

The power structure is composed of those who can have you fired or moved aside, plus those who can influence the decision. The DM, now your boss, certainly can demote or dismiss you. So can the DM's boss and the boss of the DM's boss, depending on the importance and visibility of your new position. These members of the power structure are easy to identify. The lobbyists, the group that does the influencing, take a little more effort to uncover. For you to achieve full success, you must be able to recognize and influence all elements of the power structure.

One of Rushlow's Laws says, "To be successful in an organization, you have to do a good job, and the right people have to know it." One without the other is not enough. Sometimes some of the people in the power structure seem to be above this law, but my experience says that even the owner's incompetent relatives eventually get what is coming to them. Be convinced that you are certainly subject to the law:

YOU MUST DO A GOOD JOB, AND THE RIGHT
PEOPLE MUST KNOW IT.

And in order to do this, you must know who the right people are. Hence the importance of identifying the power structure before you can lay out your plan for success.

Protect Yourself

Management always does first whatever is necessary to protect its position and only then turns its attention to getting the job done. For management, as for you, the most important talent is that of survival, and managers are the consummate survivors. If the job is not being done, the manager, from a secure position, can always blame and fire someone else. That's how it is, so be prepared to protect yourself.

My mother was a strong, shy, and sensitive woman who believed that work was the key to success. She brought me up that way, and it was not until late in my career and after several hard lessons that I realized she was wrong, at least when it came to business. For example, at one company I had the task of managing a complex and far-flung organization that had grown, like Topsy, to the extent that no fewer than seventy-two forms were required to process a single customer order. A great deal of my time was spent on extended trips in the field, establishing procedures and accountability. I was not seen much around corporate headquarters.

My efforts resulted in a 15 percent increase in sales and profit in a flat market. In spite of this, my boss fired me with the explanation that "the job is not getting done." In fact, I had become the victim of a whispering campaign by one of my peers, who had convinced the boss that I was trying to knife him in the back. I knew that my detractor burned with ambition and considered me his competitor for promotion, but I had not regarded him as a serious threat. He got me because I was not paying attention. While I was out doing the job, he was playing the power structure. He obviously continued to play it well, because he became a corporate vice president, getting our former boss on the way up.

Compromise?

About now you are saying to yourself, "I'll be darned if I'll stay in a job where I have to butter up the boss to survive." I feel the same way and am not proposing that you should. However, protecting your flanks is different. Protecting your flanks is a professional necessity. You do this by determining the goals of those in the power structure, driving to meet these goals, and *letting the people in power know* that you are doing it. If this is distasteful for any reason and you cannot pursue the objectives set by those in the power structure, this is tantamount to failure on your part, and you will either have to move or be moved.

DRIVE TOWARD THE GOALS OF THOSE IN THE
POWER STRUCTURE, AND LET THEM KNOW YOU
ARE DOING IT.

If you can't do this without compromising your standards, find another job while you're still on the payroll, before you find yourself jobless and living off savings. If your standards do not mean that much, forget the whole subject. You will end up somewhere.

Lobbyists

Watch out for the people who can influence those in the power structure. My tale of the whispering colleague should warn you to be especially careful of those who are after the same recognition as you are. They may feel there is not enough recognition to go around and try for yours.

Be alert in the presence of higher-level staff members who are always hovering around. Treat the ones who try to confide in you with extra caution. Keep your eye on the longtime employees who report to you, especially if they seem very friendly with the boss. They may be building themselves up by tearing you down. If you are unfortunate enough to have someone reporting to you who was also on your interview committee, never drop your guard. This person may have voted against you and be devoted to spending the rest of *your* career with the company looking for chances to prove he was right all along.

The ones who openly spend time with members of the power structure are easy to spot, and you can be sure they are not there blowing *your* horn. But you'll have to be sensitive, suspicious, and alert to detect the clever ones who blend in. Protect yourself against all of them—never spout negatives that can be brought as offerings to those in power.

Friends and Relatives

No matter how much of an oaf he may be, you are not going to win against the boss's nephew, so avoid any contests with him. Be alert to special relationships that signal close communication with the power structure: for example, regular golf, tennis, jogging, dining, or nightclubbing dates. Maintain your safeguards. If you stick to the goals of those in power and stay away from negatives that can be reported, you will be able to trust everyone. But keep your guard up and your antennae scanning.

Palace Revolts

Stay out of all palace revolts. They may work with emerging dynasties but not in business. Even if you have inherited a boss who obviously must be removed at once before he runs the company into bankruptcy, stay out of the fray. The leaders of the revolt will be the first ones fired and *then* the incompetent manager. Management takes care of management.

Silence Is Golden, Inaction Blessed

Once you are in the new job, have figured out who's in the power structure, and are protecting yourself for all you're worth, you will have an almost uncontrollable desire to show everyone that you are Mr. or Ms. Wonderful. You can do this directly by telling everyone how great you are, or you can demonstrate it through action.

DO NOT DO EITHER.

You know the saying, "It is better to keep your mouth shut and let people think you are a fool than to open it and remove all doubt." Suppress your desire to spout profound words. Hold on to your opinions. Wait until you have been around long enough to understand your new situation and the power structure thoroughly. Your boss and your colleagues will be playing show and tell. I told you before, let them go first and stay ahead. Listen and learn all you can while sizing up the situation. As you know, there's a world shortage of good listeners, and your boss and associates will be only too glad to inundate you with their news.

Above all, never, never, never make an early forecast. Whether it concerns the number of units to be produced in a week, the earnings of the corporation for the next quarter, or the annual sales forecast, wait until you are sure of the lay of the land. And then be very conservative. Much better to have management a party to your forecast by urging you to increase it than to get it wrong in a rush of ill-founded optimism. If actions speak louder than words, then the wrong action or an action at the wrong time positively shouts.

Suppose you are the new general manager of a company with an unacceptable scrap rate. Resist the urge to wade in and solve the problem on the second day. Don't act too soon. Instead, determine the cause, consider possible solutions, pick the ones you think will help, and then think about your corrective action plan for a while before implementing it. In short, taking over in your new job should be an infiltration rather than a frontal attack. If you must do something right away, why not redecorate the lobby? Messing that up won't affect the bottom line.

Our church needed a new pastor, and we were all elated to learn that Dr. Tom, a nationally recognized authority on the Bible, had accepted the job. His last parish had doubled in size in five years, and his first official act at our church was to push out the back wall to double the seating capacity. The anticipated growth never came. In fact, attendance dropped off. Our little rural community was just not ready for his high-powered approach. Dr. Tom made an ill-advised forecast that burdened our parish with debt and caused him to move on to another assignment within two years.

But It Worked Before

Do not assume that what worked in the past will work now. This is a common mistake of the newly hired manager. Al, an associate of mine, was a successful marketing manager from the aerospace industry when he was brought into an old-line industrial company to "add new ideas." He lasted less than three years. His mistake was trying to apply the management techniques that had been highly successful for him in working with missiles and space vehicles to a company that manufactured machine tools. Most of the people in the old-line company had been there for years, and for many it was their first and only job. The organization was steeped in tradition and was not ready for space-age flip charts and fancy program plans. As I debriefed Al, it became apparent to me that:

- He had not identified the power structure.
- He had not set up a plan for survival.
- He had moved too fast.
- He had mistakenly applied techniques that had worked in the past.
- He had not listened to feedback.

- He had been victimized by the old-timers, who lobbied against him.

Beyond this, he probably had done everything right. Al turned out to be very important to that company and effected major improvements in the time he was there. In retrospect, he realized that he could have reached the same goals much sooner if he had set up and implemented a survival plan and practiced some basic diplomacy. Both Al and the company lost out through his misjudgment of the situation.

Loyalty

"The only real authority is the authority of knowledge." You already have job knowledge, as evidenced by the fact that the Decision Maker picked you as the one who would be the best at making him or her look good. You now have survival knowledge. To complete the store of know-how needed to speed you to success in your new and better job, you must understand the necessity for absolute loyalty. From day one until you receive your last paycheck, you must support your boss and company 100 percent. You owe it to them to work toward their goals for as long as they are paying you. There can be no compromise. You must never say anything derogatory about your bosses or the company, and all constructive criticism must be made directly to the appropriate person. Loyalty is one of the most important attributes for success in any job. If you can't fulfill this 100-percent loyalty requirement, you will have to leave, on either your own volition or the company's.

There is some confusion about loyalty. People sometimes think this means a lifelong commitment to work for a company: "I've worked for the company for fifteen years. It would be disloyal for me to consider another job." However, you don't build up a loyalty debt. It is not like the mortgage on a house that has to be paid off. You owe loyalty to a company only as long as you are on its payroll. If there is a better opportunity available to you, take it. This is no more disloyal than when a company makes necessary layoffs.

It can be difficult to give your full support to managers who are grossly incompetent, and you may think that the loyalty requirement can be waived under such circumstances. Never! Give these people the loyalty you committed yourself to when you agreed to work for them. (The same goes for any new boss you inherit, competent or otherwise.) In the case of incompetence, wait in the weeds until higher management makes the correction that must be made. If you are disloyal and try an end run, you will not be around to benefit from the correction when it comes. Management will protect the incompetent until it is ready to act. To repeat, management takes care of management.

You are going to experience all kinds of bosses in your career, some good and some not so good. Be kind. Being a boss is a tough job. People in this position need support and understanding. Give your boss the same support you would like to receive from those who report to you.

Keep the Pathways Open

You may have become involved with me and my book because the decision to find a better job was made by or for you. You don't anticipate that this will happen again, at least not soon. Nevertheless, keep the pathways open. Make sure your friends know where you are and what you are doing. Tell all your associates about your new position. Maintain contact with any search firms you worked with by sending them an updated resume. Your rifle-shot letters and ad responses will have produced new contacts—stay in touch with them. Keep the pathways clear in case you need them again.

Market yourself in the industry. Join a trade association. Chair a committee. Write articles on your specialty for the trade magazines. Update the data filed with your alumni association. Help the United Way. Be seen and heard. Then, in the event that you want or need a better job again, you will not have to start back at square one as you did this time.

Checklist for Success

Here is a checklist for success in your new job:

- Protect yourself.
- Listen, don't talk.
- Don't make an early forecast or rush into action. (If you must do something right away, redecorate the lobby.)
- Trust the authority of your knowledge.
- Strive for the goals of the members of the power structure, and let them know you are doing it.
- Keep the pathways open.
- BE LOYAL.

And when you are settled happily on the new career path of your choice, don't forget that I told you so.

Ed Drushlow